THE INTE
STUDENT'S
SURVIVAL
GUIDE
TO LIVING IN
NYC

Published and distributed by

ONE **TO** WORLD

One To World is proud to publish the newly edited and compiled publication, *The International Student's Survival Guide to Living in New York City*, an invaluable and proven resource for both newly-arrived and long-term resident students, interns, educators, and the New York metropolitan community and beyond! This 2009 edition includes both of our previously stand-alone publications — *Help Yourself to Housing & The International Student's Guide to Living in New York City* — creating one single publication with all of the most up-to-date and cutting edge information available today.

This is the ninth publication we have produced since the book was first launched, and we have greatly benefited from the help and advice of countless contributors over the years. We gratefully acknowledge the generations of international students, international student advisors, One To World staff members, and volunteers whose great ideas and specific contributions have made this guide possible. We also express our appreciation to our advertising sponsors for recognizing the importance of this project with their financial support.

One To World would like to extend a special thanks to Liza Stark for her tireless efforts in the overall creation of *The International Student's Survival Guide to Living in New York City*, a true labor of love!

The mission of One To World is to create global citizens and inspire a peaceful world through one-of-kind programs in classrooms and communities.

ONE **TO** WORLD

Formerly Metro International

285 West Broadway, Suite 450
New York, NY 10013
Tel: (212) 431-1195 ext. 21
info@one-to-world.org   www.one-to-world.org

Credits

Project Managers: Deborah Clifford, Katya Musacchio

Production Team: Katya Musacchio, Emily Reiss, Liza Stark

Research & Editing: Deborah Clifford, Becca Freeman, Katya Musacchio, Emily Reiss, Liza Stark, Alanna Vaughns

Immigration Information: Eugene Goldstein, Attorney-at-Law; Erika Rohrbach

Sponsors
92nd Street Y de Hirsch Residence

Educational Housing Services

Eugene Goldstein, Attorney-at-Law

New York University

OneCampusNYC.com

Sara's Homestay

Students, Interns & Young Professionals choose
92ND STREET Y DE HIRSCH RESIDENCE
Lexington Avenue at 92nd Street for extended stays in New York City

- No lease, no brokers
- 24-hour security
- Fully-furnished single and shared rooms
- Free wireless internet & weekly housekeeping service
- Communal bathroom, kitchen & laundry rooms on each floor
- Part of world-renowned cultural community center; enjoy free and discounted tickets to programs and concerts
- Discount to on-site Health & Fitness Center with pool
- Great location in Manhattan's chic Carnegie Hill district, near Central Park and Museum Mile
- Reasonable monthly rates; 30-day minimum stay

Call 1.800.858.4692 or 212.415.5660, visit us at www.92Y.org/dehirsch or email dehirsch@92Y.org

92Y Charles Simon Center for Adult Life & Learning
Lexington Avenue at 92nd Street
An agency of UJA-Federation

Contents

The Basics

ARRIVAL

John F. Kennedy International Airport (JFK)	9
LaGuardia Airport (LGA)	9
Newark Liberty International Airport (EWR)	10

NEW YORK CITY & ITS BOROUGHS

Manhattan	9
Brooklyn	10
Queens	11
The Bronx	11
Staten Island	11
Nearby New Jersey	12

GETTING AROUND

Transportation	13
Subways	13
Buses	14
Taxis	14
Car Service	14
Driving	15
Renting a Car	16
Biking	17
Chinatown Buses	17
Lucky Star Bus	17
Apex Bus	17
Fung Wah Transport Vans, Inc.	17
BoltBus	17

CLIMATE & DRESS

Climate and Dress	18

SAFETY

General Safety	19
False Friends	20
Important Telephone Numbers	20

MANAGING MONEY

Currency Exchange	21
Banking	22
Savings Accounts	22
Checking Accounts	23
Debit Cards	23
Checks	24
Travelers' Checks	25
Safe Deposit Boxes	25
ATMs	25
Credit Cards	26
Credit History, Credit Rating and Credit Checks	27
No Credit History?	27
Other Options	28
Tipping	28

The New York Housing Process

WHAT KIND OF HOUSING?

Temporary Housing & Residences	29
Dormitories & University Housing	30
Renting a Room in a Private Home	30
Apartment Shares	30
Subletting an Apartment	31
Renting Your Own Apartment	32
Checklist for Selecting Housing	33

WHERE SHOULD YOU BEGIN?

Off-Campus Housing Office	33
Word of Mouth	34
Neighborhood Resources	34
Newspapers	34
Internet Housing Resources	35
Avoiding Scams and Fraud	36
Real Estate Brokers	37

WHAT DECISIONS ARE NEEDED?

Location	37
Your Budget	38
Safety	38
Budget Worksheet	39
Checklist for Making Your Home Safe	41
Roommates	42
Space and Lifestyle	42
Expenses	42
Making a Roommate Contract	42

HOUSING LAWS

The Lease	43
"Do's and Don't's" of Signing a Lease	44
Security Deposits	44
Rent Stabilization	45
Rent Increases	45
Vacancy Allowances	45
Your Right to Have a Roommate	45
Your Right to Sublet	45
Your Obligations as a Tenant	46
Your Landlord's Obligations	47
Where to Get More Information About Your Rights as a Tenant	48

AFTER YOU MOVE IN

Setting up Utilities	49
Electricity, Gas, and Water	49
Internet	50
Television	51
Staying In Touch	52
Telephones	52
Cell Phone Use in the United States	54
Landline Telephones	55
Pay Phones	56
Fax Machines	56
Mail	57

Living Like a New Yorker

SHOPPING

Buying Furniture and Housewares	59
Department Stores	59
Food Shopping	60
Sales and Discounts	61

LIBRARIES

Libraries in New York	62

LEGAL HOLIDAYS

Observing Legal Holidays	63

HAVING FUN

What's Out There?	63
On a Budget	64
Nightlife	65

THE INTERNATIONAL STUDENT'S GUIDE TO LIVING IN NEW YORK CITY

General Survival

STAYING HEALTHY

Coping with Culture Shock	66
Medical Insurance	66
Physicians	67
Hospitals	67
Dental Care	68
Pharmacies	68
Mental Health Care	68
Women's Health Care	69

BRINGING YOUR FAMILY

Issues to Consider	69
Family Housing	70
Childcare	70
Schooling for Your Children	70
Activities for Your Spouse	71

FINANCIAL AID

Financial Aid for International Students	72

IMMIGRATION INFORMATION

Immigration Issues	73
Basic Travel Documents	75
Passport	75
Certificate of Eligibility (Form I-20 or DS-2019)	75
Visa	76
Form I-94	77
Proof of Financial Support	77
Taxes	77

LEAVING NEW YORK

Getting Ready to Leave New York	79

Appendix

RESOURCES

International Student Service Organizations	80
English Conversation Programs	81
Volunteering	81
Lesbian, Gay, Bisexual, and Transgender (LGBT) Services	82
Students with Disabilities	82
Travel in the U.S.	83

CONSULATES & MISSIONS

Consulates & Missions	84

NAVIGATING NYC

Manhattan Street Design	92
Key to Manhattan Street Addresses	93
Key to Manhattan Avenue Addresses	93

GLOSSARY

Housing Glossary	94

HOUSING LISTINGS

Short-Term Accommodations	97
Long-Term Accommodations	106
Long-Term Accommodations (Women Only)	109
Long-Term Accommodations (Men Only)	111

THE INTERNATIONAL STUDENT'S SURVIVAL GUIDE TO LIVING IN NYC

Introducing **OneCampusNYC.com**...

the one-stop resource that helps NYC college students:

- Discover NYC neighborhoods
- Compare our colleges and graduate schools
- Connect to resources including financial aid, housing, transportation, etc.

Simplify your life – visit **OneCampusNYC.com** today!

New York City Economic Development Corporation

NEW YORK CITY. MAKE IT HERE.

Michael R. Bloomberg, Mayor
The City of New York

Timmins
Val-d'Or
North Bay
Trois-Rivières
Ottawa
Toronto
Rochester
N.Y.
Albany
Pittsburgh
Hartford
New York
Philadelphia
Trenton, N.J.
Dover, DEL.
Annapolis, MD.
VA.

Most international visitors to New York City arrive at one of the area's three main airports. All three airports are operated by the Port Authority of New York and New Jersey. For airport transportation information and general information for each airport, call the Port Authority at (800) AIR-RIDE, 8 a.m. to 6 p.m. weekdays, or check out their website at **www.panynj.gov**. The Port Authority also publishes an *Airport Map/Guide* for each airport, showing the locations of parking lots, airline terminals, access routes and services; call to request a copy.

John F. Kennedy International Airport (JFK)

JFK is located in Queens, about 15 miles from mid-Manhattan. Hundreds of international and transcontinental flights arrive and depart everyday. There are several ways to get into the city from the airport: **New York Airport Service Express Bus**, which can take you via bus to one of several locations in the city for $13 – $15; the **Super-Shuttle**, a shared door-to-door van service which will take you to any address in Manhattan for around $17 – $19 (+ tolls and tip); or a regular yellow taxi (or "cab") which will also take you to any Manhattan address for a flat rate of $45 (+ tolls and tip). Alternatively, if your budget is tight you can take:

- the *AirTrain JFK* ($5) from inside any airport terminal to **Howard Beach Station**, where you can transfer to the A subway train ($2 MetroCard).

- the *AirTrain JFK* to **Jamaica Station** in Queens, where you can transfer to the E, J or Z subway train ($2 MetroCard) or the *Long Island Rail Road (LIRR)*.

For JFK Airport general information, call (718) 244-4444.

LaGuardia Airport (LGA)

LGA is also in Queens, about 8 miles from mid-Manhattan, and primarily offers domestic flights. A *New York Airport Service Express Bus* from outside any terminal costs $10 – $12 and goes to several locations in Manhattan; a *Super-Shuttle* van will deliver you to any location in Manhattan for $15 – $22 (+ tolls and tip); and a taxi into Manhattan costs between $21 – $30 (+ tolls and tip). If you're on a tight budget, you can take the M60 MTA Bus to 125th St ($2), and along the route you can connect to the 2, 3, 4, 5, 6, A, B, C or D subway trains ($2 MetroCard). If you pay with a MetroCard, the transfer between bus and subway is free.

For LaGuardia Airport general information, call (718) 533-3400.

Newark Liberty International Airport (EWR)

Newark Liberty International Airport in Newark, New Jersey is 16 miles outside Manhattan and serves both international and domestic routes. The **Olympia Trails Airport Express Bus** will take you from Newark to Grand Central Terminal, the Port Authority Bus Station or Penn Station (one way $14 / round trip $25). As with the other airports there is also a *Super-Shuttle* offering a shared door-to-door van service for $15 – $19 (+ tolls and tip), and taxis for $40 – $65 (+ tolls and tip). You can also take *AirTrain Newark* from your terminal to the Newark Liberty International Train Station, connecting to a *New Jersey Transit* (NJ Transit) train, which you can take to New York's Penn Station (34th St. and 8th Ave.) for $15.00. **Note** that you purchase your NJ Transit ticket at the airport and use it twice—once on the AirTrain and then again on the NJ Transit train on your trip to Penn Station.

For Newark Airport general information, call (973) 961-6000.

NEW YORK CITY AND ITS BOROUGHS

Manhattan

The island of Manhattan is the smallest borough, but certainly best known, since it is the heart of the cultural and commercial activity of New York City. Only 13.4 miles long and 2.3 miles across at the widest point, Manhattan is the most expensive and densely populated (1.6 million residents) of the five boroughs. It offers a wide range of neighborhoods and housing options that differ considerably in price, size, convenience, and safety. There are few bargains; most rents range from moderately to prohibitively expensive, forcing many people to seek housing in the outer boroughs. In general, the further uptown you go, the cheaper the rent prices. Neighborhoods such as Washington Heights, Harlem, and Inwood, which are the most distant from downtown Manhattan, tend to be much less expensive than those further downtown. Some pockets of lower Manhattan (specifically those near the site of the World Trade Center) offer rental incentives, such as reduced rent or no broker's fee, in order to attract tenants and revitalize the neighborhood. All subway lines except the G line run through Manhattan, and most neighborhoods are easily accessed by public transportation.

Brooklyn

With nearly 2.5 million residents, Brooklyn has the largest population of the five boroughs. One third of its residents are foreign born, and it is home to a variety of ethnic groups, including African Americans, Italians, Jews, Russians, and Caribbean Islanders. Because of the high cost of housing in Manhattan, a growing number of students, artists and young professionals are moving to Brooklyn, particularly to the neighborhoods of Williamsburg, Fort Greene, and Prospect Park area. While Brooklyn offers a wide variety of housing options, there are some areas—such as Park Slope and Brooklyn Heights—where rent prices can be as expensive as Manhattan. Some affordable neighborhoods to explore in Brooklyn are Clinton Hill, Fort Greene, Carroll

Gardens, Cobble Hill, Prospect Heights, Crown Heights, Windsor Terrace, Sunset Park, and Red Hook, among others. Linked by numerous subway lines, many neighborhoods in Brooklyn are only a short ride away from downtown Manhattan.

Queens

Queens is the largest borough, covering 108 square miles, and is also the most international, with 44% of its 2.2 million residents born outside the United States. Safe, comfortable, and convenient for shopping, Queens is largely composed of residential, ethnically diverse, family-oriented communities. In general, Queens is one of the most affordable boroughs in New York City. Average rents are significantly lower than in Manhattan and even some parts of Brooklyn, although some neighborhoods like Astoria are becoming more expensive. Popular neighborhoods in Queens include Astoria, Flushing, Jackson Heights, Rego Park, Elmhurst, Long Island City, and Woodside. Served by several major subway lines, Queens is easily accessible from Manhattan; however, despite its close proximity to Brooklyn, the two boroughs are not widely connected by subway. The G line does connect Brooklyn and Queens, but it is notorious for its repairs and consequent delays; it is also good practice to exercise extra safety precautions on this subway line late at night. Bus lines often provide a more direct route.

The Bronx

The Bronx has the distinction of being the only borough of New York that is not on an island. A largely residential area with 1.3 million inhabitants, the Bronx is home to diverse communities, including large numbers of Central and Eastern Europeans, African Americans, and Puerto Ricans. Because of its distance from central Manhattan, rent in the Bronx tends to be very affordable. The Northwest Bronx is a good area to look for housing, and the Fordham University and Italian Belmont areas are also popular with young people and students. The borough is linked to Manhattan by 15 bridges, 6 major subway lines, and 2 Metro-North Railroad lines in addition to its own extensive network of public and private bus lines. If you're attending school in one of the other boroughs, be prepared for a long subway commute. However, you might find that spending the extra time on the subway or bus is worth the reasonable rent that the Bronx can offer.

Staten Island

The city's "greenest" borough with the smallest population (fewer than 500,000), Staten Island seems a world away from the bustle and tumult usually associated with New York City. Winding streets, neat lawns, and a view of New York Harbor enhance the quiet, suburban atmosphere of Staten Island. Only the Manhattan skyline visible in the distance is a reminder that the island is New York City's fifth borough. While a rather long commute to Manhattan makes this borough a less popular place to live, the lower rent is a definite attraction. Lower Manhattan is 30 minutes away via the Staten Island Ferry (free); several express buses travel the Verrazano-Narrows Bridge that connects the island with Brooklyn. To get around on the island, there is a bus and a limited subway system.

Nearby New Jersey

Across the Hudson River a short distance from Manhattan lies another opportunity for affordable housing in New Jersey. Several cities in nearby New Jersey have attracted numerous students, young professionals, and artists. Hoboken and Jersey City, for example, are easily accessible from Manhattan via PATH trains. You might also consider Union City and West New York, both with large Latin American populations. If you are lucky, you might just find an apartment with spectacular river views of Manhattan! Before you decide to live on the other side of the Hudson, however, you may want to consider the double—and sometimes triple—transportation fares you will have to pay to commute into the city. It is also important to think about whether or not you will feel too removed from the mainstream of city life in New York.

GETTING AROUND

New York City may strike the newcomer as an intimidating place, with its crowded streets, its fast-moving pedestrians, and its "canyons" of skyscrapers. However, once you develop a basic understanding of the geography of the city and become familiar with the different transportation systems, you will quickly become more confident in your ability to navigate the city.

Manhattan streets are laid out in a grid pattern, with avenues running north and south (uptown and downtown) and streets east and west (crosstown). Fifth Avenue divides Manhattan into the east and west sides. South of 4th Street, in the older part of the city, streets follow an irregular pattern and have names instead of numbers. The other boroughs do not have the same rigid layout. Queens has a unique system; because of the large number of avenues, addresses there consist of two sets of numbers. For example, the address: **23-05 31st Avenue**
                                                                                Queens, NY
denotes house number "**5**" on **31st** Avenue at **23rd** Street in Queens.

Get yourself a good street map (available in bookstores) to assist you in finding your way around New York City's various boroughs. A great way to sample the flavors of New York City's neighborhoods is to sign up for one of the many walking tours offered on weekends. During the academic year, One To World runs excellent walking tours that are designed with international students (and their budgets) in mind. Check out our website, **www.one-to-world.org**, for details of upcoming tours. For listings of other walking tours, look in *Time Out New York*, *The Village Voice*, or *The New York Press*.

Transportation

New York City buses and subways are both run by the Metropolitan Transit Authority also known as **MTA**. For more information call **(718) 330-1234**. For a free subway map, ask an agent in any station booth. Bus maps are available on buses. The standard bus and subway fare is $2.00 per ride. To travel on the subway, you must buy a **METROCARD**, which is a prepaid travel card. To travel on the bus, you can use a MetroCard or exact change (coins only). You can purchase single ride MetroCards, but it is more convenient and economical to purchase "pay-per-ride" or "unlimited" MetroCards.

Purchasing a pay-per-ride MetroCard allows you to store money on your card. Each time you ride the subway or bus, the fare is deducted from your card. Pay-per-ride MetroCards can be purchased for a minimum of $4.00 (2 rides) and a maximum of $80.00, and are refillable. If you put $7.00 or more on a pay-per-ride card you receive a 15% bonus, giving you extra rides (so a $20.00 purchase actually covers $23.00 worth of rides). A pay-per-ride MetroCard also allows you free transfers between the bus and subway.

If you ride the subway or bus regularly, it is probably more economical for you to purchase an "unlimited ride" MetroCard, which will allow you to take as many rides as you need within a fixed period of time, for a set price.

- $7.50 for a one-day "fun pass"
- $25.00 for a seven-day unlimited card
- $47.00 for a fourteen-day unlimited card
- $81.00 for a 30-day unlimited card
- Note that if you use your card often enough, you will end up paying considerably less than $2.00 per ride—the more you ride, the less you pay.

Subways

While the New York subway may be best known for its heat (actually, in summer all the cars are air-conditioned!) and crowds, it is absolutely the fastest way to get around the city. It is a vast and sometimes confusing system, with a 100-year history dating back to separate lines that were independently built and privately managed. However, the extensive network (running from the farthest reaches of Queens to the northernmost Bronx) offers incredibly good value for the money spent, and is relatively safe, even at night.

The subway runs 24 hours a day, seven days a week. Because it never stops, service changes and disruptions sometimes occur to allow for repairs and construction, especially at night and on weekends. Be sure to look for service change information on signs posted in the stations and on the bulletin boards near the main station booth, or check the MTA website: **www.mta.info**.

If you are still unsure of the subway and how to get around, check out the website **tripplanner.mta.info/** for in-depth information on subway and bus routes. Another great intercity (and borough) resource is **www.hopstop.com**. Go here for specific directions and duration between your travel points; you have the option to choose among subway trains, walking, commuter trains, and taxis, and it gives you the cost of each. It even takes the time of day into account when calculating the trip's total time!

Buses

Buses in New York are not the fastest way to travel, but they can be a great way to see the city, and, like the subway, they run 24 hours a day, seven days a week. Separate bus maps are available for each borough. Every bus has a number indicating its route and a letter indicating the borough (M for Manhattan, Q for Queens, B for Brooklyn, Bx for the Bronx and S for Staten Island). For traveling between boroughs, particularly to and from Staten Island, express buses can be a good option. Express buses cost $5.00 per ride and are marked with an "X" before the route number; remember to purchase a roundtrip amount since there may not be convenient MetroCard machines, in which case you will have to pay with coins. It is helpful to know that if you are riding a bus at night you can be let off at any point along your route (as a safety precaution), not just at designated bus stops.

Taxis

A New York taxi will look familiar to almost every visitor to the city; its bright yellow exterior is featured in countless films, TV shows, and photos of the city. Within Manhattan, taxis—or "cabs"—are generally plentiful and relatively easy to hail at any curbside, except during rush hour (5 – 6 p.m.). All yellow cabs have **meters** that indicate the fare. The current fare is an initial $2.50 plus 40 cents per fifth of a mile, or 20 cents per minute while stopped in traffic. There is an extra $1 charge from 4 – 8 p.m. on weekdays (excluding holidays), and an extra 50 cent nighttime charge from 8 p.m. – 6 a.m. Bridge or tunnel tolls are extra. Don't forget to tip! (See *Tipping* in the "Managing Money" section.)

Taxi drivers are obligated to take you anywhere in the five boroughs or to Newark airport, and are prohibited from charging you more than the metered fee. To complain about a car or driver, or to trace lost property, call the Taxi and Limousine Commission at 311, or go online to **www.nyc.gov/html/tlc/html/home/home.shtml**.

Car Service

Outside of Manhattan, yellow cabs are not generally available on the street. Different "car service" companies offer cars and drivers who will pick you up and drive you to your destination for a fee. You can find a car service company in your area by looking in The Yellow Pages telephone directory under "car service." Call the company and tell the dispatcher where you are and where you would like to go. *Always ask what the price of your trip will be*, as there are no meters in car service vehicles. Different companies may charge different prices. Occasionally, you will have a long wait, so call ahead if you need to depart at a specific time

Some Car Companies

MANHATTAN
Delancey Car Service
(212) 228-3301

Tel Aviv Car Service
(212) 777-7777

Carmel Car Service
(212) 666-6666

BROOKLYN
Cobble Hill Car Service
269 Court Street
(718) 643-1113

Continental Car Service
(718) 499-0909

Nostrand Car Service
2946 Avenue S
(718) 339-5400

THE BRONX
Gun Hill Car Service
9 E. 213th Street
(718) 515-2600

My Way Private Cars
1872 E. Tremont Ave.
(718) 881-2222

Taxi House
346 Grand Concouse
(718) 585-5473

QUEENS
Sunshine Car Services
11105 Rockaway Blvd.
(718) 322-1800

STATEN ISLAND
Newport Car Service
2 Tompkins Avenue
(718) 720-4444

Dongan Hills Car Service
37 New Dorp Place
(718) 987-5577

Clifton Park Hill
Car Service
554 Richmond Road
(718) 442-6464

Driving

Driving a car in New York can be both costly and frustrating, and very few New York City residents choose to keep a car in the city. Parking garages are very expensive, and finding a parking space on the street is a chore; you risk having your car vandalized, and "alternate side of the street" cleaning schedules require that you pay close attention to days and hours when parking is forbidden in a particular location. Car insurance is also expensive, and heavy or grid-locked traffic is yet another deterrent.

If you do plan to drive, you will need a valid driver's license. Rules for the validity of your home-country driver's license vary by state, so check with the local Department of Motor Vehicles (DMV), Motor Vehicle Commission (MVC) or your University International Student Advisor.

New York State (NYS)

For international students in New York State, driver's licenses from all other countries are valid, and are preferably accompanied by an International Driving Permit (only obtainable in your home country). The NY DMV actually discourages international students from trying to obtain a New York State driver's license, unless you intend to permanently settle in the U.S. They require that you present a social security card (check the DMV website for acceptable forms of identification) and surrender your home country license when you apply for a NYS license.

The New York Department of Motor Vehicles
Available weekdays 8 a.m.– 4:00 p.m. (Eastern Time), except on state holidays

From area codes 212, 347, 646, 718, 917
(212) 645-5550 or (718) 966-6155

From area codes 516, 631, 845, 914
(800) DIAL-DMV (800-342-5368)

From all other area codes in New York State
(800) CALL-DMV (800-225-5368)

From locations outside the state of New York
(518) 473-5595

New Jersey (NJ)

International visitors are allowed to use their home country driver's license, accompanied by an International Driving Permit, for up to one year. However, if you will be living in New Jersey for more than 12 months and plan to drive, you are required to apply for a New Jersey license within 60 days of moving there. You don't have to surrender your home country license when obtaining a NJ license. Depending on whether your country is a member of the United Nations Convention on Road Traffic, you will be required to take certain tests in order to obtain a New Jersey license. Call the number below for a list of participating countries and required documents.

New Jersey Motor Vehicle Commission

(888) 486-3339 (from New Jersey) or
(609) 292-6500 (from outside of the state of New Jersey)

Connecticut (CT)

International visitors are permitted to use their home country driver's license, accompanied by an International Driver Permit, for up to one year. Full-time students on a student visa can use their home-country driver's license with an International Driver Permit for the duration of their stay. If you do apply for a Connecticut license, you don't have to surrender your home-country license. Only students from Canada, France and Germany are required to apply for a Connecticut driver's license if they want to drive a car, and they have to do so within 30 days of moving there.

Connecticut Department of Motor Vehicles

(860) 263-5700 (within Hartford area or outside of Connecticut)
(800) 842-8222 (elsewhere in Connecticut)

Car insurance is something else to bear in mind when buying, renting, or borrowing a car in New York. It is essential to check that you are properly covered in case of accident or theft. Some popular car insurance agencies are **Geico**, **Progressive Car Insurance**, **Allstate Car Insurance**, and **AIG Auto**.

Renting A Car

Renting cars is expensive in the city, especially if you are younger than 25. However if you are traveling out of the city with a group of friends, it may be economical to rent a car and split the cost. Try checking out car rental agencies in New Jersey or around the three main airports to find rates that are more affordable than those in the city. You can search for good bargains online, or check the Yellow Pages for car rental companies in your area.

Some popular car rental companies are **Enterprise Rent-A-Car**, **Budget Car Rental**, and **Avis Car Rental**.

Sometimes it is cheaper to rent a car through a travel agency in your home country, especially if you're from Europe. When you pick up your car in the U.S., you will have to show a driver's license from the country in which you booked the car. If you're planning a long trip, consider traveling to another state by bus, train, or airplane, and renting a car in a smaller town where rates may be much less expensive (reservations can be made from New York if you rent from a national company).

An alternative to traditional car rental companies is Zipcar, an easy and relatively inexpensive option. It allows you to reserve a car for between one hour and four days, then pick up the car at a location convenient for you. In order to become a member, however, you must be 21 years old. Prices range from $9 – $11 / hour and $70 – $77 /day on weekdays, and from $11 – $13 / hour and $90 – $115 /day on weekends. Gas and a certain amount of mileage are covered in the price (180 miles to start). In addition, they accept driver's licenses from almost every country as long as a driving record is submitted. Some universities are affiliated with Zipcar to offer cheaper prices for their students, so be sure to check before making a reservation independently. Visit **www.zipcar.com** for more information.

Biking

Biking is a great and healthy way to travel around the city, especially in the summer. The city has over 350 miles of Greenways, or trails intended for bikers and pedestrians. On these paths you can get to know Manhattan by circling the entire island. There are many places to purchase bikes—just be sure to buy a strong and secure lock as well. You can also rent bikes at various locations around New York for day trips.

For more information on trails, visit **www.nycgovparks.org/sub_things_to_do/facilities/af_bike_paths.html**.

For more information about renting bikes, visit **www.centralparkbiketour.com/** and **pedalpusherbikeshop.com/page.cfm?pageID=42**

Chinatown Buses

There are buses that run specifically from the Chinatown area in New York to many different areas on the eastern coast of the country. These buses are fantastic if you are on a tight budget since they are very inexpensive ($15 – $40 for most routes) and run frequently. Because of the popular demand for these trips, the buses fill fast. It is wise to reserve a seat and pay online before your trip.

Some Chinatown buses:

LUCKY STAR BUS
www.Luckystarbus.com
Travels between New York and
  – Boston, MA
  – Vernon, CT

APEX BUS
www.Apexbus.com
Travels between New York and
  – Philadelphia, PA
  – Rockville, MD
  – Baltimore, MD
  – Washington D.C.
  – Richmond, VA
  – Norfolk, VA
  – Atlanta, GA

FUNG WAH TRANSPORT VANS, INC.
www.Fungwahbus.com
Travels between New York and Boston, MA—runs every hour daily and every half-hour on holidays

BOLTBUS
www.boltbus.com
Fares start at $1 depending on how far in advance you buy your ticket and what day of the week you are travelling.

Travels between New York and
  – Philadelphia, PA
  – Cherry Hill, NJ
  – Washington D.C.
  – Boston, MA

New York's climate is relatively temperate; however, in summer (June–August) temperatures can exceed 90 degrees Fahrenheit (32 degrees Celsius) and in winter (December–March) can occasionally fall below 10 degrees Fahrenheit (–12 degrees Celsius). Alternating hot and cold spells are common. Expect frequent rain showers in the spring months of April and May, with occasional thunderstorms and spells of humidity in June–August. Windy snow showers and ice storms blow into New York during the months of December–March. All public buildings are heated in the wintertime, and most are air-conditioned in the summer.

Light cotton is the most comfortable fabric for summer wear, as New York can get extremely humid. In the fall and spring, heavier cottons such as denim should suffice, but woolen clothing is recommended for wintertime. A warm winter coat (preferably waterproof), scarf, gloves, and a hat are essential, and waterproof boots can come in handy. New York City skyscrapers often turn the city's streets into wind tunnels, which can make the weather seem more severe. You'll need rain gear and a sturdy umbrella that can withstand strong winds.

Clothing worn by college and university students is generally informal. For most American students, jeans are standard attire throughout the year, and can be worn at school, movies, concerts, museums, sports events and most bars, restaurants, and discos. Unlike some dress codes in other countries, there is no standardized fashion for classes. In fact, this is one of the great things about New York: people dress in a wide range of styles depending on their personality. After all, this is one of the fashion capitals of the world!

On the other hand, informal attire is usually not acceptable at fine clubs, upscale bars and restaurants, places of worship, or concert halls. In the business world dress codes remain conservative. Women typically wear suits, dresses, or formal pants, while men dress in suits and ties. Many offices have a "business casual" dress code, meaning that men can wear a less formal shirt with a sports jacket. For women, more casual skirts or pants and a shirt or sweater are appropriate. Denim jeans, shorts, and athletic wear are not considered business casual attire. "Formal attire" generally means a suit and tie for men and a nice dress for women. "Black tie" implies a tuxedo for men with dress shoes and an evening gown for women, usually with high heels or fancy flats.

General Safety

As you start to become familiar with New York City and its neighborhoods, you will begin to feel relaxed about moving around the city. New York City is much safer today than 30 years ago, but, like in any large urban area, it is important to be aware of certain things while living here. The best advice is to always be alert, but not to be afraid. And use your common sense. Here are some general tips, or "street smarts," that most longtime New Yorkers try to keep in mind:

If you know that you may be walking alone at night, map out your route beforehand and avoid dark, deserted streets. Always have extra cash available to take a cab should the need arise. When possible, try to travel with a companion. You should walk as if you know where you're going, and try not to look lost...even if you are! Avoid stopping in a public place and opening a map of the city as this will mark you as a tourist and a possible target for pick-pockets and "con artists."

You should also avoid parks after they close at dark, taking out or counting money on the street or subway, or leaving your possessions unattended, even at college libraries. Be sure to keep your handbag zipped or snapped shut while in a public place, and keep a tight grip on it! An alternative is to wear a travel money carrier, which is worn under your clothing. Leave your expensive jewelry at home or tuck it away out of sight under your clothing. Be especially alert for pickpockets on crowded streets, buses, and subways—and never carry your wallet in the back pocket of your pants.

Stay away from card games, fortune tellers, and strangers promising you "good deals." These and other "con artists" will try to trick you into giving them money, but you can't win!

As in any large city, New York has many beggars, or "panhandlers," often located around subway entrances, on subway cars, or around ATM machines. You should never feel pressured to meet a demand for money simply because of someone's aggressive behavior or persistence. Panhandling is, in fact, illegal on the subway, although you will see it often.

Try to avoid riding the subway alone late at night; it's usually better to take a bus or a taxi. If you do use the subway at night, wait for the train near the station booth or in an area where other people are standing. Avoid empty or unlit cars, and ride in the middle car near the MTA official.

If you suspect that someone is following you, go into the nearest store or crowded area; don't enter your building alone if you think someone is behind you. If you do happen to become the victim of a robbery, do not resist. Be prepared to give up your valuables willingly to avoid the greater danger of being hurt. Remember that if you stay calm, you are unlikely to be injured.

Keep in mind that most university campuses have their own security force and generally offer a free escort service for students who prefer not to walk alone late at night. Contact your school to find out what services are available to you, and don't hesitate to use them when you need to.

False Friends

We know that you will make many new friends during your stay in New York City. As a newcomer, you will find yourself getting invited to take part in all sorts of different organizations, from school clubs, to religious groups, to fraternities or sororities, to intramural sports teams. The great majority of these organizations and groups will be legitimate and well meaning. However, there are also illegitimate organizations, often known as "cults," that use high-pressure recruiting tactics to bring in new members, and you will need to exercise caution to avoid organizations like this.

Cults often appear to be religious groups but sometimes masquerade as therapy groups, political organizations, or even business or management-training groups. They may pressure you into joining by making you feel guilty if you say "no," or by making you think that there are tremendous advantages to becoming a member. Members may also try to make you give up your religion, contribute money, or help them recruit other members. In the worst cases, cults can disrupt your life, force you to cut ties with your family and friends, and perhaps even pressure you to quit school and give up career plans.

Remember that cults often look for people who are unusually vulnerable. International students are often considered targets because they know you may be lonely, struggling with a language barrier, or unaware that these groups are potentially dangerous.

This, of course, does not mean that every active student club or organization is a cult. You will have to use your judgment and make careful decisions. Don't join a group without asking questions about it first. And don't hesitate to ask your international student advisor for advice.

Important Telephone Numbers
Keep these handy by your phone.

Emergency (police, medical, fire):	911 (24 hours a day, free from any telephone)
New York City Info & Service:	311
Poison Control:	(800) 222-1222
Crime Victims Hotline:	(212) 577-7777 in Manhattan or (800) 621-4673
Police Sex Crimes Hotline:	(212) 267-7273
Physicians on Call:	(212) 737-1212
Con Edison Gas Emergency:	(212) 683-8830
Terrorism Hotline:	(888) NYC-SAFE (692-7233)

The basic unit of U.S. currency is the dollar ($1.00). Coins are minted in denominations of one cent (penny), five cents (nickel), ten cents (dime), twenty-five cents (quarter), and fifty cents (half-dollar). One dollar coins (a silver one named after Susan B. Anthony, an early women's rights activist, and a golden one featuring Sacajawea, a Native American heroine) exist but are infrequently used, except as change in subway and train ticket machines and postage machines. Bills (paper money) are printed in $1, $2 (very rare), $5, $10, $20, $50, $100 denominations. Be careful—all the bills are the same size and color! Be wary of counterfeit (fake) bills, especially at bars and clubs—make yourself familiar with the special features (such as watermarks and texture) of authentic bills so that you will know how to spot counterfeit ones.

Currency Exchange

Before you open a bank account, you will probably need to exchange currency or travelers' checks in order to get you started. As you know, exchange rates fluctuate daily. Many major banks, as well as companies like American Express or Thomas Cook, offer currency exchange services. Outside banking hours, you'll have to use a private exchange office. Be sure to ask about the rate and any commission charges before you change money. You will need to present identification, such as your passport, each time you exchange currency.

If you bring a bankcard from your home country, be sure to find out any service fees before you use it in the U.S., as there could be an unwelcome surcharge.

In order to arrange for transfers of funds from your home country to the U.S., you can either request a bank draft to be forwarded through the mail (but it may take up to three weeks for this money to clear and become available to you) or request an electronic transfer of funds directly into your U.S. account. You will most likely be charged a fee for both services.

For a quick currency converter, check out **www.xe.com**.

Banking

Most students opt to open a local bank account in order to avoid carrying large sums of cash or travelers' checks. A bank account is also useful in helping you keep track of funds more closely.

Because service and fees vary from bank to bank, you should research the banks in your area to find the one that best suits your needs. **Some banks offer special student accounts with lower service charges than regular accounts,** or your school may have a special arrangement with a local bank. Ask at the International Student Office, and take advantage of these services. Banks that have an arrangement with your school are more likely to accept your school ID in place of a social security number when you set up your account. (Some banks require that you have a social security number in order to set up an account. Others will require you to show your passport and either a second ID, proof of address, or a letter from your school. Check with your local bank to find out which supporting documentation you should bring to open an account.)

Banks are generally open from 9 a.m. to 5 p.m. on weekdays, but increasingly you will find branches that are open early or on weekends. Almost all are closed on federal and state holidays. Almost every bank has automated teller machines (ATMs) that allow you access to your account 24 hours a day, seven days a week. Most banks now also have online banking, allowing you to access account information, transfer funds between accounts, pay bills and make inquiries outside of your bank's normal hours and from anywhere where internet access is available.

Questions to Ask When Deciding on a Bank:

- Does the bank offer any special student accounts?
- What are the monthly fees?
- Do I have to keep a minimum balance in my account?
- Is there a limit on the number of transactions I can make per month?
- Does the bank charge an extra fee for use of ATMs that are not their own?
- Does my bank have a number of branches in my area/in Manhattan?

Once you decide on a bank, you will need to choose what type of account(s) you wish to open. The following is a basic overview of the two main types.

Savings Accounts

Savings accounts enable you to earn interest on funds that you don't need right away. The rate of interest will depend on the bank and the type of account you have chosen. When you open your account, most banks will begin to send you a monthly statement that will detail all your transactions and any interest you have accrued. Some banks, however, will issue you with a passbook instead, in which your deposits and withdrawals are recorded. You must bring the passbook with you each time you wish to make a deposit or withdrawal. The interest you earn on your money will usually be recorded in the book four times a year (quarterly).

You can withdraw money from your savings account in cash or in the form of a bank check. You can also generally transfer money from your savings account to your checking account as needed. Deposits to your account can be made in cash or by check, but you may have to wait 5 – 20 days to withdraw money deposited by check (depending on the size of the check and where it originates). Be sure to ask how long it will take checks to "clear" (be processed by the bank) before you open an account.

Checking Accounts

Checking accounts enable you to withdraw your money frequently in the form of

- checks to pay bills and / or send payments in the mail
- cash for daily expenses
- a debit card with which you can purchase goods and services

A checking account can help you keep track of how you are spending your money. You must keep a careful record of every check you write, all deposits that you make, and every cash withdrawal. At the end of each month, you have the option of receiving a bank statement in the mail or online. Both will include a summary of all your deposits and withdrawals for the past month. You can also check the status of your checking account at any time through a secure page of the bank's website.

Get in the habit of "reconciling" or comparing the monthly statement from the bank with your own records, to make sure they match. Remember that checks can sometimes take a while to "clear." Be sure to deduct any service or check fees, and to add any interest you have earned. If you discover a discrepancy between the bank's records and your own, take your checkbook and statement to the bank.

Debit Cards

Debit cards are linked to your checking account and can often be used in place of a credit card. Payments made with a debit card are deducted from your checking account balance, either immediately or within 2 – 3 days. It is important to retain your receipts and to remember what you have spent so that you will know if a charge is still outstanding. Debit cards with a credit card logo can be used in most stores, online, and over the telephone. Debit cards without a credit card logo will require you to enter your PIN at a store terminal, and cannot be used online or over the telephone. Although you can usually use your debit card to withdraw money from your savings account at an ATM machine or to transfer money from your savings to your checking account, remember that your debit card is only linked to the funds in your checking account when you use it to make a purchase. Make sure you have enough money in your checking account before using your debit card.

Checks

Checks are one way to pay expenses such as rent, telephone bills, and other household expenses. Banks often return "cleared" (processed) checks or photocopies of them to you; these give you proof of payment if a question arises about whether a particular bill has been paid. Another way to pay these expenses is through online banking. Most banks allow you to pay credit card bills online through a process know as online bill-pay. Most store credit cards, telephone companies (including cell phones), computer companies have account numbers that can easily be stored with your bank and then automatically paid monthly. Check with your landlord to see if he or she is a part of any online rent payment system. You can make all your payments online!

You will often be asked to show a photo ID if you are paying by check at a store. If you write a check without sufficient funds available in your account to cover it, your check will "bounce." Don't do it—you will be fined by your bank and probably also by the company to which you wrote the bad check, and your credit rating will suffer. This makes it doubly important for you to keep careful records of all your transactions. For information on your *credit rating* and *credit history*, see page 27.

Always write checks in ink, never in pencil. Always be careful to sign your checks and date them correctly (remember that the American way of writing a date is month / day / year). The following diagram illustrates the correct way to write a check.

It is a good idea to have your address printed on your checks when you initially order them; your phone number is not necessary. Checks generally include a line at the bottom for a "memo." Use this to write your account number when you are paying a bill or any other note about your payment.

When someone else writes you a check, you need to "endorse" it for payment to your account by signing your name on the back in the appropriate section. Note that writing "for deposit only" (and your account number) on the back prevents others from cashing your check in the event that it is stolen.

John Doe
123 Main St
Anywhere US 10111   Date   *01/01/2008*

PAY TO THE ORDER OF   *The Sandwich Shop* $ *8.15*

Eight and 15/100   DOLLARS

Your Bank
456 Main St
Anywhere US 10111

MEMO

1: 123956789 1:   100100239"1   0790

Travelers' Checks

These checks are especially useful to cover your temporary living expenses before you've established your bank account, as well as for trips, as they are accepted virtually everywhere around the world. You must keep a record of each check number, separate from the checks; in the event that your checks are stolen, your report of these numbers will enable you to receive replacement checks. Travelers' checks can be purchased at most banks for a small service fee.

Safe Deposit Boxes

Safe Deposit Boxes are available at most banks. For a small fee, you can rent a box in which to store valuables, such as official documents, valuable jewelry, etc.

ATMs

Automated Teller Machines, more commonly called ATMs, are a service that most banks provide, offering you banking privileges 24 hours a day, seven days a week. Each bank with which you have an account or accounts will issue you an ATM card and ask you to choose a personal identification number (PIN). Most ATM cards also double as debit cards. Customers are not limited to using ATMs at their own banks. The symbols on your card (NEW YORK, Cirrus, Visa) indicate the various systems through which you are able to access your bank account—look for ATMs with matching symbols.

By "swiping" your card at an ATM and entering your PIN into the machine, you will be able to perform the following transactions:

- Withdraw cash
- Make deposits of cash and checks to your own account (only at branches of your own bank)
- Transfer funds between your accounts
- Obtain your account balance

Always be sure to get a receipt and make note of all ATM transactions in your checkbook in order to keep a record of your balance at all times.

Note that some ATMs outside your home bank may charge a service fee of $1.25 to $3 that is automatically deducted from your account. You will be informed of this fee before you complete your transaction. Try to avoid using ATMs that charge extra fees, as these can add up quickly. Check with your bank to see if they charge an *additional* fee for using an ATM that is not affiliated with them. For example, if the ATM has a surcharge of $1.50 and then the bank charges you $2.00, you could be charged $3.50 for taking out $20! As a rule, ATMs located in commercial stores such as delis or bars have a higher surcharge than ATMs at bank branches.

ATMs are very convenient, but a word of caution: be careful when using these machines. Even though many ATMs are located in well-lit lobbies with doors that automatically lock behind you, avoid visiting ATMs alone late at night. Never give anyone else the opportunity to use your card, even if they offer to help, and be sure that no one watches you enter your PIN number. Make sure you always exit your account and collect your ATM card and receipt after you have completed all transactions. Put away your cash, card, and receipt immediately, before heading back to the street.

Credit Cards

Credit cards such as Visa, MasterCard, and American Express enable you to buy goods and services on "credit" by signing a receipt saying that you promise to pay the amount of the sale. In order to get a credit card, you must apply through your bank or another institution that will examine your financial records and assign you a "credit line," meaning the maximum balance you can carry on your card based on your income. (As a full-time student, you are unlikely to qualify for a large credit line.)

Shop around for a credit card. You may find yourself showered with offers of credit cards, some requiring payment of an annual fee, others "free." Interest rates and penalties vary. Ask lots of questions and compare offers before deciding which card to get. Some American Express cards require you to pay in full each month; however you may carry a balance on your Visa or MasterCard as long as you pay the minimum payment each month. But be careful! You will be charged a hefty interest rate that varies from company to company on the charges you carry over. It is very easy to accumulate finance charges on your card and end up being unable to make the payments. And if you miss one or more payments, your card is likely to be canceled. Use credit cards with discretion!

In addition to the convenience, you may find it necessary to obtain a credit card in order to establish a credit history (a record of on-time bill payment which can help you qualify for further credit for "big-ticket" items, such as a car or a mortgage). Also, keep in mind that in order to do some things, like rent a car, you must have a credit card. It is also a good idea to have a credit card in case you find yourself in an emergency situation. A credit card can also be used like your bankcard in an ATM to obtain fast cash (although at a high interest rate so this is not advised). Keep all receipts from your credit card purchases and reconcile them with your statement each month.

You should be extremely cautious when using your credit card (or a debit card) online. It is important to check that you are using a "secure site" that guarantees the privacy of the transaction and the safety of your credit card number before you pay for something over the Internet. Do not send your card number by email or enter it on an unsecured site. If you do so, you risk having your card number stolen and misused.

If you bring a credit card from home you should make sure that it is possible to pay your bill from here, or make careful arrangements for someone in your home country (such as a relative) to transmit payments every month for you.

Always make sure to completely fill out and sign all credit card (and debit card) payment slips, and to keep them as records of your purchases. If you pay for a meal or other service with a credit card or debit card, you may receive a payment slip with a price, a space for entering a tip, and a space for entering the total price (original price + tip). Always fill out these spaces before signing a payment slip of this kind, or you risk someone entering a higher tip or higher total than you may wish to pay. If you do not wish to pay for a tip using your credit card, simply put a line through the space for tip on the payment slip and enter the original price in the space for the new total.

For information on obtaining a credit card:
www.ftc.gov/bcp/conline/pubs/credit/choose.htm

If Your Credit Cards Are Lost or Stolen:
American Express (Amex) (800) 221-7282
MasterCard   (800) 622-7747
Visa   (800) 847-2911

Credit History, Credit Rating, and Credit Checks
Your **credit history** is a track record that shows you have been able to pay back loans and pay your bills in a timely manner. Landlords or brokers, banks or other companies may insist on running a credit check on you before they agree to rent an apartment to you or offer you other services.

There are three major **credit bureaus** (Equifax, Experian, and TransUnion) that track your ability to pay back loans and bills. Every time you pay, or fail to pay a bill— whether it is to your school, your bank or your phone company—this information becomes available to the credit bureaus. When a company runs a credit check on you, they contact one of these bureaus to find out how good or bad your record is. If your **credit rating** is good (for example, over 600 on a scale of 300 – 900), it means you have a track record of re-paying loans or paying bills promptly. Your credit rating suffers when you pay a bill late or don't pay it at all. It can also suffer for other reasons—like having too many credit cards at once, or going into overdraft on your checking account.

From the time you first **establish credit** in the U.S., it takes time to secure a high score on your credit rating. This means you are only likely to benefit from establishing credit if you plan to be in the U.S. for a couple of years. In the meantime, even if your credit record back home was good, landlords or companies may decline to do business with you until they have a way of guaranteeing your reliability through a standard credit check.

There are several ways of establishing credit and then building and maintaining a good rating in the U.S. Speak with a bank representative about secured credit cards and other options when you open a bank account. Always make sure to pay your school, utilities and other bills on time, and to reconcile and close your accounts before you leave the U.S. (especially if you ever plan to move back in the future!).

No Credit History?
There are ways around not having a credit history in the U.S. You can avoid the services that require a credit check—for example, by subletting rather than leasing your own apartment or by using university housing. In some cases, landlords may agree to let you sign a lease if you have a guarantor—someone with a good credit rating who will take responsibility for your rent if you fail to pay it. Others will require a large deposit, or ask for several months' rent in advance.

Other Options

Money Orders serve the same purpose as checks, but do not require a checking account. You can purchase these with cash at a post office, and also at large supermarkets or other stores in your neighborhood, for a small fee. Money orders can be written in any denomination you wish.

Check Cashing / Financial Services Locations are independent companies that accept cash payments for household bills. They can also cash certain checks for you if you don't have a checking account. These services usually charge a large fee, however, and should only be used in emergency situations.

Tipping

Tipping for service is a standard practice throughout the United States, especially in restaurants and bars where tips are not so much a "bonus" for waiters and bartenders, as an expected part of their income. In New York bars, a dollar tip per drink is a good rule of thumb. In restaurants, the usual tip is **15% to 20%** of the bill. Because New York City adds an 8.625% tax on all purchases, a quick trick for calculating the amount of the tip in a restaurant is to double the tax. Remember that the size of the tip should be based on the service provided. You are not required to tip 15% for service that was inadequate, but on the other hand, it is expected that you will tip extra when you receive special service. If you eat out in a group of eight or more people, some New York City restaurants automatically add a 15% – 20% tip, also called a "service charge" or "gratuity," to your bill. Always check your bill to see if a service charge has been applied before you add a tip.

There are other service providers who are commonly tipped. For hairdressers and taxi drivers, a 10% – 15% tip is appropriate. Movers are generally also tipped. For bellhops and porters, a tip of a couple dollars per bag is standard. For more info, visit **www.tipping.org**.

WHAT KIND OF HOUSING ARE YOU LOOKING FOR?

In a large and densely populated city like New York, finding a comfortable place to live is the first step to survival in the big city. Getting settled in safe and affordable housing can be an important factor in enjoying your life in New York. The metropolitan area offers a diverse array of housing options from which to choose, but your search for housing can be a challenging and sometimes complicated process. This section is designed to advise and assist you in this process, but remember that ultimately you are the best judge of your own housing needs and which situation will work best for you. As you get started, the first thing you should consider are the types of housing available:

- Temporary Housing and Residences
- Dormitories and University Housing
- Renting a Room in a Private Home
- Apartment Shares
- Subletting an Apartment
- Renting Your Own Apartment

Temporary Housing and Residence

Be aware that it can take some time to find a suitable place to live, especially in New York's tight housing market. You will probably need a temporary place to stay while you are conducting your search. Regular hotels are expensive, but there are other options. If you are a student your first step should be to check with your foreign student advisor or campus housing office to ask if there is an affordable facility near your school where you can stay until you locate permanent housing. If you already have friends or family in the New York area, discuss the possibility of staying with them before you arrive.

Other temporary housing options include YMCAs, youth hostels, and the temporary residences that are listed in the appendix. These places provide rooms for anywhere from one night to one month, and some for even longer. If you are interested in staying in a residence on a longer term basis, you can look into the residences listed in the appendix as well. Many of these residences fill up very quickly, so you should make arrangements for your stay well in advance.

Always call, fax, or email first—you will save time and energy!

Dormitories and University Housing

Many colleges and universities provide dormitories or other housing for their students. Usually both single and shared rooms are offered, as well as a variety of services such as meal plans, laundry facilities, and TV or study lounges. Most dorms house men and women in the same building, but not usually on the same floor. Choosing university housing is a good solution if you want to move in quickly and live in a ready-made community with other students. It also enables you to avoid the responsibilities of signing a lease and furnishing and maintaining an apartment.

There is no better way for a newly arrived student to adjust to life in New York City than to live with other students. Many newcomers report that living in campus housing provides a sense of community that can otherwise be hard to find upon first arrival to New York City. Living in a dormitory, at least during your first year, can help you feel more at home in your new surroundings.

Keep in mind, however, that few New York City campuses have sufficient housing for all their students who request it. If you are interested in this option you will need to act quickly and reserve a room well in advance of arriving in New York City. There are often long waiting lists and rooms get taken quickly! Be sure to keep yourself knowledgeable and updated about your university's housing process.

Renting a Room in a Private Home

Local residents occasionally rent an extra room in their home or apartment to students at a nearby campus. Usually the room will be furnished with a bed, dresser, and desk, but it may or may not include a private bath. You might also have permission to use the kitchen. For information about renting a room in a private residence, contact your school's Off-Campus Housing office to inquire whether they keep a list of such accommodations or check notices posted on campus bulletin boards.

Though relatively inexpensive, this type of living situation requires careful consideration. Remember that you may have to adjust your lifestyle to accommodate the person or family with whom you will be living. For instance, if you are a smoker and the owner of the house doesn't allow smoking, then this isn't the right situation for you. On the other hand, you may find that you have much in common with your new "family" and this could be the start of a rewarding friendship. The best way to avoid major problems is to get to know your prospective housemate(s) before you make the decision to rent the room. Think about your needs and the specific circumstances very carefully before you make your decision.

Apartment Shares

A share refers to a situation in which you move into a space (apartment, loft, house, etc.) that has already been rented by another person or persons, and agree to divide the responsibilities and payment of rent and bills. You may or may not have your name added to the lease or be asked for a deposit. As with any roommate situation, it is important to discuss any expectations you might have, and agree on ground rules at the beginning. One benefit of moving into a share situation is that there might be more flexibility concerning how long you agree to stay. With an apartment lease, however, you must take responsibility for a complete year's rent even if you will be leaving after nine months. Notices of shares can be found posted on campus bulletin boards, on and offline, and in many newspaper classified ads.

Subletting an Apartment

You may choose to sublet an apartment from a tenant who temporarily leaves the city and plans to return to the same apartment after a period of time. For example, an actor living in New York may get a temporary three month job in Hollywood. Instead of moving out of his or her apartment, the tenant may choose to sublet it to another person. This means that someone else, a "subtenant," can live in the original tenant's apartment and use all the furniture and kitchenware until the primary tenant returns.

This is very common in New York City, but you should be cautious if you agree to sublet an apartment. A subtenant's rights aren't always as clear as those of a primary tenant. During a sublet the original tenant takes full responsibility for all obligations under the lease, continues to pay the rent to the landlord, and reserves the right to reoccupy the apartment. You should be sure that you are dealing with a reliable person... and that you, too, are reliable. Above all, you should be certain that the apartment you decide to sublet can be sublet on a legal basis. A sublet that does not comply with the law may be grounds for eviction of both you and the primary tenant.

A reliable tenant follows legal procedures when subletting his apartment to you. To sublet an apartment, the tenant must first obtain permission from the landlord. In general, a landlord is obligated to give his permission unless he can prove that you would be a "bad" subtenant. For example, the landlord may require information about you and your ability to pay the rent. Generally, you will pay rent to the tenant, who will then forward the rent to the landlord.

Another item a landlord may request from the tenant and subtenant is a copy of the sublease. The sublease is a written contract that states:

1. the condition of the apartment and its furnishings;

2. the duration of the sublet; and

3. your responsibilities as a subtenant.

Be sure to keep a copy of the sublease for your records.

The primary tenant should remove all valuable items from the apartment before you move in. If it is a short-term sublet, the tenant should make specific arrangements with you about mail delivery and telephone messages.

Other points to remember about subletting:

- While the primary tenant is away, the conditions of his/her lease cannot be changed without his/her consent.
- If you are subletting a furnished apartment, the primary tenant is not allowed to charge you more than 10% above the legal rent. (This can be verified by looking at the tenant's lease.)

- You will probably have to pay a security deposit of from 50% to 100% of one month's rent. This amount may vary depending on the duration of the sublet and the furnishings provided, as well as the condition of the apartment. This money should be deposited into a savings account at the bank and returned to you when you vacate the apartment provided that you have left the tenant's home and furnishings in good condition.

For more information on how to sublet your own apartment, see Chapter 4 .

Renting Your Own Apartment

Having your own apartment is probably one of the ultimate "New York Experiences." Although it can be a frustrating, time-consuming process to find an apartment, most long-term residents prefer this option because it provides maximum freedom, space, and privacy. There are no curfews, no rules about guests, and you can decorate your space however you like!

Looking for your own apartment requires patience and determination. Most people find that they must look at many apartments before they find one that they like and can afford. In searching for your own apartment, you may encounter obstacles such as expensive rents, high broker fees, and enormous competition, especially in Manhattan. You will need to be persistent and even aggressive about following up leads and placing phone calls. Once you find something you like and can afford, you must act on it right away. There is no guarantee that you will get the first apartment that appeals to you.

Once you have found a suitable apartment, you will have to go through a complicated approval process, which involves filling out an application, providing references from people who can vouch for your reliability (you can ask your foreign student advisor, an employer, or previous landlord, professors, family friends, and/or relatives), documenting your financial resources, and submitting to a credit check (proof that you have a history of paying your bills on time). There is often a small, non-refundable fee for processing an application / credit check. As a newly arrived student, you may not have any credit "history" and thus, you may need to provide a guarantor. A guarantor is a person (in the U.S.) who provides a written statement of agreement to pay your rent in the event that you fail to do so.

Note: If you do not have a guarantor in the U.S., your landlord may require a larger security deposit from you.

To be prepared to make a quick decision, it is helpful to have the following items with you when you go to inspect an apartment:

1. Checkbook / travelers' checks for any required fees or deposit
2. Photo ID (passport or driver's license)
3. Credit application information (name, address, and phone number of references and guarantor)
4. Bank account information (account numbers and recent statements, if available)
5. Verification of income

Checklist For Selecting Housing

Here are some things to consider before you sign a lease!

☐ How secure is the building? Is there an intercom system or a doorman? Is the front door securely locked? Is the entryway well lit? How secure is the apartment? If the apartment is on the first or top floor, or is accessible by a fire escape, are there gates on the windows?

☐ Is it in a convenient location? Consider access to transportation and necessary services like shopping, laundry, etc.

☐ How noisy is the apartment? Traffic noise or nearby trains, schools, hospitals, or fire stations can all make for a noisy location.

☐ How many flights of stairs will you have to climb if there is no elevator? Will a great view compensate for extra physical labor?

☐ Is the ventilation adequate? Does the apartment receive sunlight for at least part of the day?

☐ Is the closet and storage space adequate?

☐ What kind of bathing facilities does the apartment have?

☐ Are the electrical and plumbing working and properly maintained? How many electrical outlets are in each room?

☐ Do a stove and refrigerator come with the apartment? Are both in good working order?

☐ Are there visible physical defects, such as cracked plaster or leaking faucets? (If so, write down everything that is wrong and try to get the landlord to sign a written agreement that the defects will be repaired. If he/she refuses, send the list to the landlord via *registered mail* and request a *return receipt*[1], before you get the keys.)

WHERE SHOULD YOU BEGIN YOUR SEARCH?

Off-Campus Housing Office

If you are affiliated with a university, it is always a good idea to see if your school has an Off-Campus Housing office which posts apartment listings from local landlords, notices of sublets or rooms in private homes, and listings for roommates and shares. Off-Campus Housing is usually located in either the student affairs office or in the Residence Life / On-Campus Housing office; you will need to show your student ID in order to gain access to the office. The services of this office are free and generally provided by student employees.

---

[1] A return receipt provides a green postcard with the recipient's actual signature by mail or a proof of delivery letter arriving as a PDF attachment that includes an image of the recipient's signature by e-mail.

Also be sure to check their website for updated postings. Be aware that housing listings change frequently, so you should look for recent updates many times a day. Using the Off-Campus Housing office can be one of the most convenient and least expensive ways for students to find housing.

Word of Mouth

Believe it or not, word of mouth can be one of the best ways to find a place to live in New York City. The more people you talk to about your search, the more likely it is that someone will give you information that will lead you to what you are looking for—they may even have friends who are looking for a roommate. Expand your network by telling as many people as possible that you are looking for a place to live, which neighborhood(s) you are interested in, and what your price range is. Some housing seekers even print up fliers or cards to share with friends and acquaintances to remind them of their search.

While not easy, it is occasionally possible to find an apartment by walking through a neighborhood where you think you would like to live and talking to building superin-tendents or doormen to see if they have apartments available. You might also talk to the mail carrier, local residents, or shopkeepers to see if they know of vacant apartments in the area.

Neighborhood Resources

As you conduct your search, don't forget to check notices for apartments on bulletin boards at your own school, at a nearby campus, or in neighborhood stores. Some schools restrict the use of such bulletin boards to their own students. Off campus you can often find housing notices on bulletin boards at local supermarkets, restaurants, bus stops, bookstores, copy services, or laundromats. You can also use these bulletin boards to post your own notice stating what type of apartment you are looking to rent or share. Your card or flier should include your name (first name only), a phone number where you can be reached and/or an e-mail address, and the type of apartment or living situation you are seeking. For personal safety reasons, do not include your full name or the address of your temporary residence.

Newspapers

Another good way to look for an apartment is through listings in the classified advertisements or the real estate sections of local newspapers.

The *New York Times*, published daily, has the largest number of listings of apartments in the city, especially in the "Real Estate" section of its Sunday edition (distributed Saturday morning to home subscribers). Listings are also available online through the *Times'* website **www.realestate.nytimes.com**, and you can sign up for email alerts that will send you details of properties matching your criteria.

The *Village Voice*, a weekly newspaper that is published every Tuesday evening in Manhattan (Wednesday in the other boroughs), also has a large selection of apartments in its classified ads section. Since the *Voice* is read by many students and young people, it contains cheaper listings than many other publications. The *Voice*'s listings are so popular, however, that apartment seekers often compete to get early access to the ads as soon as they are available. The *Voice* posts its listings on line at **www.villagevoice.trulia.com/NY/New_York** every Tuesday afternoon at 1:00 p.m. A subscription to an email service sending advanced, personalized listings is available for a fee. For details, visit their website or call at (212) 475-3300.

Other major metropolitan area newspapers are also worth checking, especially their local editions. *Newsday*, for example, publishes a special Queens edition that has a good listing of available housing in Queens (**www.newsday.com**). If you are looking for housing in Staten Island, pick up *The Staten Island Advance*, (**www.silive.com/advance**) which can be found at the South Ferry terminal in Manhattan, as well as on Staten Island. And in New Jersey, the *Jersey Journal*, (**www.nj.com/jjournal**) the Record (**www.bergen.com**) and the *Star Ledger* (**www.nj.com/starledger**) are good sources for local apartment listings.

Throughout the city, there are many smaller community newspapers that contain real estate listings for specific neighborhoods. Often these publications are free; you can find them in supermarkets or in special boxes on the street. Remember also that New York is an international city, with a great many ethnic neighborhoods, and many of these also have their own native-language newspapers. You can find a listing of these resources at the website, **www.housingnyc.com/guide/classifieds.html**.

School newspapers can also be a good source of information on housing opportunities, especially notices submitted by students who are looking for roommates to share rental costs with them.

Regardless of which newspaper(s) you consult, it is important to obtain the paper as soon as it is distributed, and then to call or visit the apartments promptly, because desirable places are taken quickly. **Be aware that many newspaper listings are placed by real estate brokers, rather than by owners or landlords. Brokers charge a fee to find an apartment for you (see page 37).**

Internet Resources

In addition to the newspaper websites mentioned above, there are a number of housing resources on the web that are immensely useful; even if you decide not to pursue this avenue, browsing them will let you know what is out there. If you are affiliated with a university, the first place you want to look is on your school's website. Many campus housing offices offer online housing resources and post their listings, which means you can get a headstart on your search—even from home!

There are many "public" online housing resources and forums as well, such as **www.roommates.com** or **www.sublet.com**. The most notable of these is Craigslist, where you can find local classifieds and forums that are community moderated for more than 500 cities in over 50 countries worldwide. On their website (**www.craigslist.org**), you can search apartment listings, find furniture, even look for a part-time job. The New York City Rent Guidelines Board (RGB) hosts a website (**www.housingnyc.com**) which provides important information about rental housing in NYC. There you can find an apartment guide, research reports, rent guidelines, and the tenant's rights guide—there is even an email question and answer service available through this site.

Avoiding Scams and Fraud

While these housing sites are usually the most convenient in accessing a wide range of possible options, there are some important precautions to take if you decide to go this route. As the popularity of these sites has increased with prospective renters, their corresponding popularity among scammers has risen greatly. As a result of New York's high pressure housing process, con artists are able to fool more prospective tenants with fake housing postings. Through these scams, they mislead potential renters into sending them money but do not follow through on their side of the housing process and are usually never heard from again after they receive your check. In general, the best way to avoid this situation is to use your common sense. Below you will find a list of more specific tips from craigslist.com to follow as you navigate your search.[2]

Common Sense Rules to Work by:

- **Deal locally with people you can meet in person**—follow this one simple rule and you will avoid **99%** of scam attempts.

- **Never wire funds via Western Union, Moneygram** or any other wire service—anyone who asks you to do so is a scammer.

- **Fake cashier checks and money orders are common**, and banks will cash them and hold YOU responsible when the fake is discovered weeks later.

- **Craigslist (and most other housing forums) are not involved in any transaction**, and does not handle payments, guarantee transactions, provide escrow services, or offer "buyer protection" or "seller certification."

- **NEVER GIVE OUT FINANCIAL INFORMATION** (bank account number, social security number, eBay / PayPal info, etc.).

- **Avoid deals involving shipping or escrow services and know that only a scammer will "guarantee" your transaction.**

Personal Safety Tips to Follow:

- Insist on a public meeting place like a café.

- Tell a friend or family member where you are going.

- Take your cell phone.

- Consider having a friend accompany you.

- **Trust your instincts.**

For more information and examples of scam attempts, visit
www.craigslist.org/about/scams.html.

---

[2] www.cragslist.org/about/scams

Real Estate Brokers

Many apartments in New York City are rented through real estate agents, or brokers, who charge a fee to find you an apartment. This fee, which is rarely negotiable, can range anywhere from one month's rent to 10%–18% of the annual rent. For example, for an apartment that costs $1,000 per month (or $12,000 per year), a broker's fee of 15% would total $1,800; you would pay this in addition to the first month's rent and the security deposit required by the landlord.

Since cheaper apartments can be hard to find, and brokers earn larger fees on more expensive rentals, a broker may try to persuade you to accept an apartment that is more expensive than you can afford. In working with a broker, be prepared to insist that you see only apartments that are within or close to your price range.

If you decide to use a broker, be sure the fee is payable only after the agency has found an apartment and you have signed a lease. Some agencies charge a referral fee (anywhere from $100 – $250) that entitles you only to look at their lists of available apartments; it is up to you to visit and negotiate for the apartments yourself. Paying for these lists can be risky because there is no guarantee that the listings are exclusive or even up to date.

WHAT DECISIONS DO YOU HAVE TO MAKE?

As you are beginning to look for housing, there are a number of decisions you need to make. The more advance planning you can do, the more effective and successful your search will be.

Location

How far away from your school or work are you willing to live? Your rent could be substantially lower if you're willing to travel a little further, particularly if your school or office is located in Manhattan. Take a look at subway or bus maps to see what transportation options are available in each area you are considering.

New York City is divided into five districts called boroughs: Manhattan, Brooklyn, Queens, Staten Island, and the Bronx. Manhattan is the commercial and cultural center of the New York metropolitan area; rents here are correspondingly higher than in the outer boroughs or in nearby New Jersey. Convenience is a big factor in housing cost, so the areas that are closest to Manhattan are usually more expensive than those farther from the city.

It can be very helpful to take a friend along for advice when you are looking for an apartment in an unfamiliar neighborhood. If you are seriously considering living in an area, it is a good idea to spend the day walking around as if it was your own—think about how it might feel to live there. Check One To World's website (**www.one-to-world.org**) for our One To World Walk schedules, or have a look at the *New York Times* "Weekend" supplement or the "Around Town" section of *Time Out* magazine.

Your Budget

Before you can make a decision about where to live, you need to think very carefully about your budget and how much you can afford. Create a monthly financial worksheet before you begin in order to project how much you can spend on housing. See the page at left for a suggested budget worksheet that will help you estimate your income and expenses. As a general rule, it is recommended that you try to spend no more than $1/4 - 1/3$ of your total monthly income on rent. In New York this can be especially difficult to achieve and you may have to compensate in other areas.

It is a good idea to open a checking account at a local bank as soon as you can. It helps if you have a credit history—having a checking account will start building one right away. Otherwise you will need to carry cash or travelers' checks in U.S. dollars so that you are ready to make required payments for a security deposit, the first month's rent, etc.

Safety

Make safety a high priority when looking for a place to live. The best way to judge an area is to visit it yourself and see if you feel safe and comfortable there. Keep in mind that neighborhoods in New York City can change significantly from block to block, so rather than judging an area by its name (Chelsea, East Village, etc.), it's better to walk around and evaluate the surroundings yourself. Walk to the nearest subway station— would you feel comfortable walking this route both during the day and late at night? Talk to shopkeepers on the block. If a shopkeeper tells you that he or she has been robbed in the last month, chances are that an apartment in this neighborhood may not be very safe. In general, it is good to have many eyes watching the street; a well-lit, busy street is usually safer than a dark, private street. Be sure that the front door of the building is locked and the entry hall well lit. If you can't afford an apartment building with a doorman, look for other safety features nearby: a doorman next door, a 24-hour shop or restaurant nearby, or a police station.

At Home

Here are some safety precautions New York City residents should keep in mind:

- **Call the police at 911 in the event of a crime, fire, or medical emergency**, whether you are directly involved or simply a witness. For non-emergency situations (such as reporting a disturbance or the discovery of a robbery) call 311.

- **Keep your door locked at all times.** When moving into a new house or apartment, consider changing all the locks. Most locksmiths recommend a "drop" or "dead-bolt" lock on all doors. Ask a locksmith, hardware store, or your superintendent for advice. Should you lose your house keys, immediately change the locks. Do not leave an extra key under your doormat, in a mailbox, or in any other accessible place.

- **When you come home, have your keys ready in your hand as you approach your door.** If your building has an unattended lobby or hallway, never let a stranger follow you into the building after you have unlocked the outside door.

BUDGET WORKSHEET

Income (Annual)		
Scholarship/Grant	$	
Loan	$	
Employment Income	$	
Personal or Family Funds	$	
Total Annual Income		$

Annual Expenses

Apartment		
Broker's Fee	$	
Security Deposit	$	
Electricity Deposit/Installation	$	
Telephone/Purchase and Installation	$	
Moving Costs	$	
New Locks/Purchase and Installation	$	
Furnishings	$	
Household Items	$	
Subtotal		$

School		
Tuition/Fees	$	
Books	$	
Other	$	
Subtotal		$
Total Annual Expenses		$

Monthly Expenses

Bills		
Rent	$	
Electric Bill	$	
Gas Bill	$	
Cable/Internet Bill	$	
Cell Phone Bill	$	
Landline Telephone Bill	$	
Subtotal		$

Daily Life		
Groceries	$	
Laundry	$	
Entertainment	$	
Personal	$	
Miscellaneous	$	
Subtotal		$

Transportation		
MetroCards	$	
Other	$	
Subtotal		$
Monthly Expenses x12 (Your annual expenses)		$

- **When someone comes to your door, always ask who is there and be sure of their identity before you open the door.** Never "buzz" anyone into the building whom you don't know.

- **Your landlord is legally required to provide a functioning smoke detector in your apartment.** Make sure to change the battery at least once a year; contact your superintendent for assistance if you suspect the detector is not working.

- If your apartment is located on the ground floor or the top floor, or can be accessed from a fire escape, **invest in window gates or install window locks**. (Be sure to check with your superintendent, as New York City fire regulations prohibit certain types of window gates that open onto fire escapes.)

- **If you plan to be away from home for several days, cancel your newspaper delivery and have the post office hold your mail or have a friend collect it for you.** A full mailbox or a stack of newspapers beside your door is a clear sign to a burglar that no one is home, making your apartment an easy target. If you have an answering machine, make sure that your message is not too informative— saying "We're not here right now" is offering too much information to potential intruders. Instead say, "I can't get to the phone right now." Avoid offering any personal information (especially your address and credit card number) over the telephone.

- **Record the serial numbers of your valuables** (such as a television, laptop, desktop, stereo, or iPod) so that in case of theft they can be readily identified and returned to you if they are recovered. Keep a master list of the numbers of all your credit cards, your passport and any travelers' checks, saved in a place that is separate from where you store these items. Should any of these items get lost or stolen, report the loss immediately to the appropriate authority.

Checklist For Making Your Home Safe

- Always change the locks of the former tenant. You never know who may have a copy of the key.

- Invest in the best when you buy new locks; you can take them with you when you move. A good lock has three components: 1) a drop or dead bolt, 2) a pick-resistant cylinder, and 3) a guard plate over the cylinder.

- If your apartment is located on the ground floor or the top floor, or can be accessed from a fire escape, window locks (and, in some cases, window gates) are especially important. Ask a neighborhood locksmith, hardware store, or your building superintendent for advice on securing your doors and windows. (Be sure that any gates on your window can be opened from the inside in case of emergency.)

- Locate your local police station (precinct office) and keep the telephone number in a handy place. Your local precinct may also be able to offer you recommendations on locks, window gates, and alarms, as well as other safety tips for your particular neighborhood.

- Keep your door locked at all times.

- Don't give your keys to anyone. Don't put your name and address on your keys or key ring! And, never leave an extra key under your door mat, in a mail box, or any other publicly accessible place.

- Report lost or stolen keys promptly to the building owner or superintendent and have the locks changed immediately. If your apartment is broken into, report it to the police.

- List only your last name and first initial on your doorbell, mailbox, and in the telephone book. If you wish to be unlisted in the telephone book, you can do this for a fee when you set up your account.

- Never open your door without knowing who is on the other side. Most apartments have a peephole in the door that enables you to see who is outside. Always ask visitors to identify themselves and to provide proof of identification. Never "buzz" anyone into the building whom you don't know.

- Make sure you are provided with one or more smoke detectors. Landlords are required to install these safety devices in each apartment, except for apartment houses with water sprinkler systems. Remember to change the battery in your smoke detector at least once a year. It is also advisable to consider purchasing a carbon monoxide detector. Both items can be purchased at a local home or hardware store.

- In case of a blackout or other emergency, it is prudent to keep water, canned food, can opener, candles, first aid kit, flashlight (with batteries) and a battery powered radio in your apartment.

- Finally, protect your belongings from damage (or loss) due to fire or theft by obtaining renter's insurance. A listing of insurance companies can be found in the Yellow Pages of your telephone directory.

Roommates

Sharing an apartment is a common solution to the problem of high rents in New York. You may not have considered this before, but many students and young professionals find people like themselves to share the high costs of living in the city. Entering into a roommate situation does require cooperation and sharing, so be sure to choose a roommate very carefully. Here are some things to think about before making such a commitment:

Space and Lifestyle

With the high cost of living in New York, space can be a luxury, but before agreeing to share housing with one or more roommates, evaluate your possessions and your lifestyle, and think about your personal priorities. For instance, the lifestyles of students and professionals can be drastically different in their schedules and routines. A studio might be fine for one person, but two people living in a single room might find the situation intolerable. In a shared situation, the kitchen and bathroom facilities should be available to everyone. Usually the living room is also shared space where roommates receive guests and socialize, but in some cases this may need to be sacrificed to make room for a roommate to sleep. Think in advance about your personal needs for privacy or a quiet area for studying.

Expenses

Rent and utilities are normally divided by the number of roommates, though rent may be prorated depending on the size of each room. You may be asked to pay an additional one month's rent as a security deposit (see page 44 for more information). If there is a shared telephone, bills are divided equally for basic monthly service, but each roommate is expected to pay for his/her own long distance calls. Remember that if one roommate moves out without paying his/her share of the rent, the landlord has a right to collect the rent from the tenants who remain in the apartment.

Making a Roommate Contract

Before moving in together, it's a good idea for you and your roommate(s) to draw up a written contract establishing how your joint home will be run. At the end of the contract, you can renew your agreement if all roommates are still happy with the situation. However, if one roommate wants to move out before the contract expires, written notice should be given one month in advance; be sure to state this in the contract. It is also common courtesy for the roommate who is leaving to help in the search for a replacement roommate to share the rent.

When writing up a contract, think about covering these items:

- **Rent & Utilities:** What is everyone's share? If the landlord requires a single check, which roommate will be responsible for writing it? Who will pay the security deposit? How and when will the security deposit be returned? Remember that if you are the primary person on the lease, you will be held responsible.

- **Space:** Who will occupy which room? How will you divide up closet or drawer space? What are the rules for use of the common areas (i.e. kitchen, living room, bathroom)?

- **Household chores:** Who will take responsibility for cleaning which space, and on what schedule?
- **Meals:** Will you share food, shopping and cooking responsibilities? If so, how will you split the costs and the work?
- **Noise:** What hours can the TV be on? How late can music be played?
- **Overnight guests:** Is it permissible for boyfriends/girlfriends to stay over? How about other guests?
- **Other considerations:** What will be your policy on smoking? Keeping pets?
- **Moving out:** If one of you decides to move, how much notice must be given? Must the departing tenant find an acceptable substitute?

It is best to put your understandings in writing. Oral agreements are too easily forgotten or misinterpreted after the fact.

There are several ways to find roommates. This process in New York often includes interviews and screenings of the potential roommate to make sure they find the right person. Craigslist has an entire section of their site devoted to apartment shares and roommates. There are also professional roommate agencies that can introduce you to potential roommates, but they often charge a hefty fee, with no guarantee of success. Generally, for students the best advice is to check your campus housing office, post on the campus listserv, or simply ask around.

WHAT DO YOU NEED TO KNOW ABOUT HOUSING LAWS?

The Lease

A **lease** is a written contract, which defines the terms by which a particular apartment is rented. It is written by the landlord and presented to the tenant for signature. Since a lease is a binding legal document you should carefully review it before you sign. Make sure you understand all the language stipulating the terms of the lease. After it has been signed, it is too late to make changes.

A lease should contain the following information:
- the name and address of the landlord and tenant
- the amount of rent and the date each month the rent is due; most landlords allow for a "grace period" that allows you to pay rent up to 5 days late
- the number of tenants
- the term of the lease (when it begins and ends)
- who pays the utility bills (electricity, gas, and heat): the landlord or tenant
- who is responsible for repairs and what cosmetic or significant structural changes the tenant can make to the apartment

Occasionally landlords offer apartments on a month-to-month basis, rather than on a one or two year lease. In this situation the arrangement may be terminated by either party provided that written notice is given at least 30 days before the next rent payment is due.

These are the DO's and DON'T's of signing a lease

DO discuss and negotiate any problem areas in the lease before you sign it; be sure to write your initials beside all changes that you and the landlord make in the lease.

DO make sure that you receive a copy of the lease with both your signature and the landlord's signature on it.

DO make sure that all the provisions of the lease are legal. Clauses that prohibit children or overnight guests are NOT legal; check with a tenants' association or a lawyer if you have questions about your lease.

DO remember that you are legally responsible for the payment of rent quoted in the lease.

DO find out what the rules are about such things as keeping a pet, disposing of garbage, making noise, subletting, etc.

DO find a safe place to keep the lease. You may want to consider renting a safe deposit box at the bank as a very secure way of storing important documents.

DON'T rely on oral agreements. Only written agreements in a lease are legally binding.

DON'T sign the lease until you are satisfied that you understand everything in it, including the legal language.

DON'T sign the lease if there are blank spaces. Cross out all blank spaces before you sign so no one can make any new changes.

DON'T feel pressured into signing the lease before you've had time to read it over slowly and carefully.

Note: It is difficult to break or alter a lease once it is signed, but if your circumstances change unexpectedly and you need to leave your apartment before the lease expires, it is worth trying to speak with your landlord to ask if special arrangements can be made. In some cases, the landlord may be willing to let you leave on 30 days notice, although you may have to forfeit your security deposit or agree to find a subtenant.

Security Deposits

Upon signing a lease, you will have to pay a security deposit of up to one month's rent to your landlord before you move into your apartment (note: this requirement may be increased to three or more months' rent if you are an international student without a guarantor). The landlord is required to place your security deposit in an interest-bearing bank account, and you should be credited yearly with the current rate of interest on this account minus a one percent service charge. When you sign a renewal lease, the landlord may require that you increase the amount of the security deposit to equal the new monthly rent. Your landlord is entitled to use your security deposit to pay for any damages (beyond normal "wear and tear") to the apartment during your occupancy. Otherwise, your deposit is returned to you when you move out, assuming your rent has been paid in full.

Rent Stabilization

Rent stabilization is a special New York City law that protects tenants in certain apartments. Rent stabilization applies to buildings constructed between 1947 and 1973 that contain six or more units and are not co-ops or condos. This law means that the city government controls the price that the landlord can charge. Before you sign a lease you should find out if your building is rent stabilized. To learn more, visit www.dhcr.state.ny.us or call (212) 961-8930.

Rent Increases

If you live in a rent stabilized building, your landlord can increase your rent only by a fixed percentage each time you sign a new lease. When you first move in, your rent is based on a fixed percentage over the price that the former tenant was paying. The law says that the landlord must show you a copy of the former tenant's lease, **but you must ask to see it**. You may choose to sign a lease for one or two years. The exact percentages of allowable increases change each year and are determined by the Rent Guidelines Board. Visit **www.HousingNYC.com** or call (212) 385-2934 for more information.

Vacancy Allowance

A vacancy allowance is a one-time fee that the landlord can charge a new tenant when they move into a rent stabilized building. The legal amount for a vacancy allowance also changes each year. This is in addition to the normal annual rent increase.

Your Right to Have a Roommate

An apartment is rented to whoever signs the lease and his or her immediate family members, including a spouse, children, parents, or siblings. A tenant living alone has the right to invite one additional occupant to share the apartment. The landlord's consent is not required, but you **must** notify the landlord 30 days after the roommate moves in. Occupants (i.e. those whose names are not on the lease) do not have the same rights as tenants.

Your Right To Sublet

As a tenant, you have the right to sublet your apartment to a subtenant. To sublet, the tenant must obtain permission from the landlord. If you decide to sublet your apartment to another person, you should make a written contract with that person. Remember that you are responsible for the actions of your subtenant, even when you are away.

In obtaining the landlord's permission, s/he cannot unreasonably withhold consent. If the landlord consents to the sublet, the tenant remains liable to the landlord for the obligations of the lease. If the landlord denies the sublet on reasonable grounds, the tenant cannot sublet and the landlord is not required to release the tenant from the lease. If the landlord denies the sublet on unreasonable grounds, the tenant may sublet. If a lawsuit results, the tenant may recover court costs and attorney's fees if a judge rules that the landlord denied the sublet in bad faith.

These steps must be followed by tenants wishing to sublet:

1. The tenant must send a written request to the landlord by certified mail with a return-receipt requested from the Post Office. The request must contain the following information:

    a. The length of the sublease

    b. The name, home and business address of the proposed subtenant

    c. The reason for subletting

    d. The tenant's address during the sublet

    e. The written consent of any co-tenant or guarantor

    f. A copy of the proposed sublease together with a copy of the tenant's own lease, if available.

2. Within 10 days after the mailing of this request, the landlord may ask the tenant for additional information to help make a decision. Any request for additional information may not be unduly burdensome.

3. Within 30 days after the mailing of the tenant's request to sublet or the additional information requested by the landlord, whichever is later, the landlord must send the tenant a notice of consent, or if consent is denied, the reasons for denial. A landlord's failure to send this written notice is considered consent to sublet.

4. A sublet or assignment which does not comply with the law may be grounds for eviction.

In addition to these sublet rules, there are additional requirements limited to rent stabilized tenants. For specific information on these and additional subletting clarifications, visit The New York City Rent Guidelines Board at **www.HousingNYC.com**.

Your Obligations as a Tenant

In renting your own apartment, you must adhere to certain requirements and etiquette. Here are some things to keep in mind.

As the tenant you must:

- Take legal responsibility for paying the rent each month for the full term of the lease; this means that if the landlord requires you to sign a 12-month lease, you must pay for all twelve months even if you move out after the school year (9 months) ends.

- Pay your rent promptly on the date stipulated in the lease.

- Keep the apartment in good condition.

- Dispose of garbage and recyclable materials in accordance with the landlord's instructions.
- Obtain the written consent of the landlord before making structural changes in the apartment, such as painting or attaching shelves.
- Be considerate of your neighbors and do not make too much noise.
- Leave the apartment in its original condition when you move out.
- Supply the apartment with your own furniture and kitchenware (unless you have rented a "furnished" apartment).
- Follow correct subletting protocol should you choose to sublet.

Note: If you violate certain provisions of the lease you can be legally removed from the apartment.

Your Landlord's Obligations

By law, your landlord must:

- Provide heat in your apartment from October 1st to May 31st.
- Provide hot and cold running water year-round.
- Maintain the public areas in and around the building, collect the garbage, provide lighting in the public spaces.
- Repair your apartment.
- Paint your apartment every three years.
- Provide a bathtub or shower, a toilet, and a kitchen sink, inside your apartment.
- Maintain a safe, weatherproof building that is free of rats, mice, and bugs; it should be livable, safe, and sanitary.
- Install smoke detectors that are clearly audible in any sleeping area.
- Furnish a locked mailbox with the tenant's name on it.
- Install a peephole in your apartment door, so that you can see visitors without opening the door.
- Install a chain-door guard on the entrance door of your apartment to permit for partial opening of the door to see visitors.
- Install mirrors in each self-service elevator in order to see if anyone is on the elevator before you get on.
- Have access to your apartment, with sufficient prior notice, to provide repairs or services.
- Be permitted to enter your apartment, without any notice, in case of fire.

Where to Get More Legal Information About Your Rights as a Tenant

NONPROFIT ORGANIZATIONS

Citizens Housing & Planning Council

42 Broadway, Suite 2010
New York, NY 10004
Tel: (212) 286-9211
www.chpcny.org
Email: info@chpcny.org

CHPC is a nonprofit, nonpartisan policy research and advocacy organization specializing in housing, planning, and economic development issues in New York City.

Metropolitan Council on Housing

339 Lafayette Street, #301
New York, N.Y. 10012
Tel: (212) 979-6238
Hotline: (212) 979-0611 (open MWF 1:30–5:00 p.m.)
www.metcouncil.net
Email: active@metcouncil.net

This organization works to preserve and expand affordable housing in New York City. It is a membership-based group that provides information and assistance on rent stabilization, housing regulations, etc. and helps with problems you may have with a landlord or real estate broker.

GOVERNMENT AGENCIES / DEPARTMENTS

Department of Housing, Division of Code Enforcement

New York Government Citizen Service Center
311
www.nyc.gov/html/hpd/html/pr/violation.shtml

To contact the Department of Housing, call 311—this center is open 24 hours a day, seven days a week to report code violations such as lack of heat, hot/cold water, electricity and apartments in disrepair, and faulty plumbing. Use this resource after you have first approached your super or the building's managing agent about the problem.

The New York City Rent Guidelines Board

51 Chambers Street, Suite 202
New York, NY 10007
Tel: (212) 385-2934
www.HousingNYC.com
Email: ask@housingNYC.com

The NYC Rent Guidelines Board is the agency that establishes rent adjustments for all rent-stabilized apartments in NYC. Their website provides comprehensive, up-to-date information on the New York City housing market, along with a variety of resources to help tenants and landlords understand their rights and obligations.

Website features include:

- an articulate facts page, as well as email questions and answers
- the New York State Attorney General's "Tenant's Rights Guide"
- "Apartment Guide" containing tips on finding apartments and online listings
- housing "fact sheets"
- other general housing information.

WHAT DO YOU NEED TO DO AFTER YOU MOVE IN?

Setting Up Utilities

Electricity, Gas, and Water

Water is generally provided at no extra cost to you, but gas and electricity are considered utilities. Some landlords include the cost of electricity and gas in the monthly rent, while others do not. If your landlord does not provide these services, you will have to make arrangements directly with the utility companies to have your gas and electricity turned on.

MANHATTAN, THE BRONX, AND PARTS OF QUEENS

Call Con Edison for both gas and electricity.
Tel: 1-800-752-6633
www.coned.com

BROOKLYN, STATEN ISLAND, AND OTHER PARTS OF QUEENS

Call Con Edison for electricity only.
Tel: 1-800-752-6633
www.coned.com

KeySpan Energy Delivery provides gas there.
Tel: (718) 643-4050
www.keyspanenergy.com

NEW JERSEY

Call Public Service Electric and Gas Company (PSE&G) for both gas and electricity.
Tel: 1-800-350-7734 for general enquiries and 1-800-436-7734 to report an emergency (such as a gas leak, power outage, loss of heat, etc.)
www.pseg.com

LONG ISLAND

Call Long Island Power Authority (LIPA) associated with KeySpan Energy Delivery for both gas and electricity.
• **Gas:** Tel: 1-800-930-5003 for billing and general enquiries
and 1-800-490-0045 for emergencies.
• **Electricity:** Tel: 1-800-490-0025 for billing and general enquiries
and 1-800-490-0015 for emergencies.
www.keyspanenergy.com

Even if the electricity and gas are already turned on in your apartment when you move in, you must call the proper companies to have the account registered in your name as of the date of your move. In some cases, you will be required to visit the company in person and bring a notarized copy of your lease with you. You may also have to pay a deposit in addition to a service charge for having the utilities turned on.

Internet

The Internet is one of the most popular resources for researching information about countless topics as varied as the news, weather reports, world maps, the entertainment industry, etc. It can also be the most inexpensive way of communicating with your friends and family across the world. With the advent of free webmail services provided by companies such as Yahoo and Google, anyone can obtain an email account.

Services

Most likely you will be entitled to a free email account and Internet access through your university. However, if you are unable to access the Internet at home through a university account, you may want to consider subscribing to an Internet service.

You can choose between different types of connections, such as dial-up, DSL, cable, and wireless. Dial-up and DSL both use your telephone line; however, DSL is much faster and allows you to use your phone line to make calls and be connected to the Internet at the same time. A cable connection also allows you to use your phone and be online simultaneously, and is faster than dial-up. If you plan to have cable television, you should inquire to see if there is a discount for getting both services at the same time. Rates can be as low as $10 per month for a dial-up connection (plus whatever your phone company charges for time on the phone line) or $30 for DSL or cable (unlimited user time) or $50 for wireless internet. Almost all telephone providers offer package deals with Internet access for discounted prices; make sure to inquire where applicable. Here are two of the main internet service providers (both also offer cable and phone services):

Time Warner Cable
www.timewarnercable.com/n00ynj/
1-800-OKCable (652-2253)

Verizon
www.verizon.com
1-800-VERIZON (1-800-837-4966)—For new service, changes to existing service, and billing questions (Monday – Friday, 8:00 a.m. – 6:00 p.m.)

WiFi

WiFi is the abbreviated term for wireless technology that connects computers, phones, PDAs, game consoles, etc to the Internet. Many cities throughout the U.S., including New York, are undertaking initiatives to provide free wireless Internet to its populace within the next few years. Until that happens, however, there are many public and private spaces with free WiFi service, such as Bryant Park or Union Square Park.

Skype

Skype is a computer software program that allows you to make telephone calls via the Internet. In recent years this method has become one of the most popular and effective ways to keep in touch with friends and family without paying high international calling costs. After downloading and installing the program, you can choose the type of service you want depending on your needs and budget:

- **Skype-to-Skype Calling**—Users of the program can call each other and certain other numbers at no cost. So if you and a family member or friend both have Skype, you can call them for FREE through this program.

- **SkypeIn**—For $30 per year users can obtain a SkypeIn phone number that allows people outside of the Skype network (i.e. non-users) to call you directly through this line. They also offer a voicemail option for this service.

- **SkypeOut**—Skype users can make regular calls to cell phones or landlines for approximately $.02 per minute

You will need to purchase a headset (you can find quality headsets for about $15) and obtain a webcam if you want to video conference. Aside from video calling, users can also engage in conference calling between multiple parties, instant messaging, and file transfers.

Go to **www.skype.com** for more information or to download the program.

Television

New York City is served by various national networks, several local channels, and a public broadcasting system. All these channels are free and require no special installation. However, reception in most parts of the metropolitan area may be extremely poor without a "cable" connection.

Along with improved reception, cable subscribers have access to many channels including Cable News Network (CNN), MTV, and many foreign language broadcasts. The monthly fee for basic cable service varies. For an additional charge, you may include access to specialized programming such as sports or movie channels. Many cable companies offer package deals combining television, phone, and Internet service for less money than it might cost to purchase them from separate companies, so be sure to shop around. Each neighborhood of New York City is served by particular cable companies. The major companies are Time-Warner (**www.twcNYC.com**), Cablevision (**www.cablevision.com**), and RCN (**www.rcn.com**)—check their websites to find out if they provide service in your area.

Staying In Touch

Telephones

Most tenants usually opt to use their cell phone as their main line of contact instead of installing a landline. A cell phone is much more convenient and consolidates your costs. Telephone service is never included in the rent: you will have to make your own arrangements when you want to connect telephone service, and you will have to purchase or rent a telephone.

To Make a Call

Phone numbers in the United States consist of seven digits plus a three-digit area code. Your telephone directory has a listing of every area code in the U.S. To make any call in New York City, local or otherwise, you must first dial 1, then the area code and the number.

212	**Manhattan**
646	**Manhattan or cell phone**
917	**Manhattan or cell phone**
718	**Brooklyn, Bronx, Queens, Staten Island**
347	**Brooklyn, Bronx, Queens, Staten Island or cell phone**
516	**Long Island (West)**
631	**Long Island (East)**
201	**Northern New Jersey**
973	**Northern New Jersey**
914	**Westchester and Rockland Counties (New York State)**

The codes 800, 822, 833, 844, 855, 866, 877, and 888 before a telephone number mean that the call you are making is toll-free (you will not be charged a fee).

To Dial Internationally

In order to dial internationally, you must first dial 011, then the country and city codes, and finally, the number you wish to reach. To find out a particular country code, dial 0 to speak to an operator or look in the White Pages telephone directory under "International Calling Codes." If you wish to call New York from abroad, the international country code for the United States is 1.

Calling Cards

In many cases, international calling cards—available at local delis and newsstands throughout the city—can provide one of the cheapest ways to call home. These are prepaid cards with an ID or PIN number that you enter to access your calling credit. You can usually buy them for values of $5, $10, or $20. There are many different brands; some work only for specific countries and some end up being a great value for a specific country or region, but less of a bargain for others. Shop around for a calling card that will work for your country and offer good value. Some stores provide charts showing the rates to specific countries for each card.

For most cards, the number of minutes you have for each call depends on how you use the service. There is often a connection fee, which means that making many short calls uses up more minutes per card than making a few long calls. Most cards give you the option of dialing a local number or a free (800) number, from which you must then enter your PIN number to access your credit. You should dial the local number if you have a landline with cheap or unlimited local service, as this will often give you more minutes per card. However, if you are calling from a pay phone, the free number may be a better deal. Finally, some cards will automatically deduct money from your credit if it is not used within a specific time frame. It can therefore be of better value to buy $5 cards frequently, rather than $20 cards from time to time.

To Find a Telephone Number of a Person or Business
Each region publishes two main telephone directories each year: the White Pages and the Yellow Pages. The White Pages is a complete alphabetical listing of all persons and businesses with listed telephone numbers in the immediate area. In most cases, addresses are also included. For privacy reasons some people choose not to have their numbers listed (this requires payment of an extra monthly fee). The front pages of the White Pages list important emergency numbers. Look here to find the number of the local fire department, police precinct, and poison control hotline, and make note of them.

The Yellow Pages is a directory of businesses and services, listed by category. This directory makes it easy for you to locate services or products you need in your immediate area. For example, to search for a drugstore in your area, look under "Pharmacies." The Yellow Pages can be located online at **www.superpages.com**, and both the Yellow and White Pages at **www.anywho.com**. To get a complimentary copy of a telephone directory, call your local telephone business office.

Another way to locate the phone number of a residence or a business is to dial Directory Assistance at **411**. If you need assistance in finding a number outside your area code, dial **1 + the area code + 555-1212**. Whenever possible, check the telephone directories before calling Directory Assistance, since you will be billed for each inquiry.

There are also a variety of "short messaging services," or SMS, that can help you find information about people, businesses, weather, translations, and more through your cell phone. One option is Google, which has free SMS. To use it, send a text message with your inquiry to "Google." For example, "**weather** new york," "8 usd **in** rubles," "**movies** (zip code)," etc. Go to **www.google.com/intl/en_us/mobile/default/sms/index.html** for more information.

DIAL 911 to report a fire, crime, car accident, or any other emergency, whether you are directly involved or simply a witness.

Cell Phone Use in the United States

With the recent surge in technology over the past decade, cell phones have become the primary method of personal contact. Most Americans today, especially students, young professionals, and city dwellers have replaced their traditional landline with a cell phone.

Cell phones work a little differently in the United States than in other countries. To use a cell phone, you need a phone as well as a wireless service provider, through which you buy a calling plan. You can buy phones in various places, but make sure that the phone will work with the wireless service provider you would like to use. The wireless service provider connects your phone to a wireless network, allowing you to make and receive calls.

Some phones, GSM phones, have SIM (Subscriber Information Module) cards that hold the subscriber's phone number and settings that are necessary for the phone to function with a particular service provider. GSM phones that are sold in an "unlocked" condition can have the SIM card reprogrammed for use on different wireless service providers. Most phones are non-GSM and contain a service provider lock (SP-lock). This prevents you from using your phone with a different service provider in the future. Even non SP-locked phones may not be useable on a different wireless network.

Types of Calling Plans

Contract (Monthly) Plans: With this plan you pay a fixed amount at the end of each month, and you have a contract that typically lasts 1 to 3 years. For this fixed amount you get a certain number of minutes each month, often at a lower rate and with additional features. With this calling plan you are committed to a service provider (carrier) and plan for the length of the contract. If you did want to cancel your contract and/or switch carriers, you would have to pay a large fee (up to $200).

Prepaid Plans: With prepaid plans, pay-as-you-go or no-contract plans, you must pay up front for the minutes you will use before you use them. These plans often have higher rates than contract plans, but there are no deposits, cancellation fees, or contracts, so you can stop using this plan without any fee. Typically, minutes are bought in fixed dollar amounts of $10, $20, etc. This plan is a good choice if you only want a phone for emergency situations or only need it for a couple of months, since the cards can expire, and the unused amount will be lost.

Data Plans: Data plans can be in conjunction with or separate from your main wireless calling plan. A data plan allows you to send and receive e-mails, text messages (SMS short message service) or picture messages (MMS multimedia service). It may also allow you to download ring tones and games, or access the Internet (using a mini-browser designed to work with text-only versions of sites such as Yahoo, MSN, Google and CNN).

A Word of Caution: Popular Promotions and Pitfalls

Promotions are used to entice consumers to buy a calling plan, but it might not always be a good deal. Make sure the features below would actually save you money before you sign up for a related promotion or sign a contract.

- Free phone
- Unlimited local calls
- Reduced monthly fee for two to six months
- Unlimited local calls between carrier subscribers
- Unlimited local calls during specific hours, such as from 5 – 7 p.m. on weekdays
- Online specials
- Discount if you buy a bundle of mobile, local, long-distance, cable TV or satellite TV services from the same provider
- Automatic enrollment—Sign up for one feature and get another automatically with an additional fee, even if you don't want the other one.
- Upgrade on contract renewal—Your contract might be automatically upgraded with more features and fees when it is renewed.
- New feature extends contract term
- Pressure into buying features or services you won't use

The above information was based on the websites below:

www.mobilook.com/CellphoneBasics.asp

www.mobilook.com/GuideToMobilePhoneCallingPlans.asp#top

Please visit them for additional information about cell phones, as well as cautionary tips when purchasing a cell phone or calling plan.

Landline Telephones

Installation

Your local phone company will install service in about one week. You will have to pay a security deposit, as well as a one-time installation charge that will appear on your first telephone bill. See the "Basic Home Telephone Service" section in the beginning of the White Pages of the telephone directory for details. When you establish local service, you must also choose a long distance provider. Take the time to research the long distance companies to see which plan is best for you.

In the New York metropolitan area, call Verizon for general information on telephone installation at (718) 890-1550. In New Jersey call 1-800-427-9977 (in-state) or 1-800-755-1068 (out of state). For telephone service or repairs, call 1-800-275-2355 (New Jersey) or (212) 890-6611 (New York). Or visit their website at **www.verizon.com**. For a complete list of other local telephone service providers, consult the White Pages of the telephone directory.

Local Service

Before you order your telephone service, read the "Basic Home Telephone Service" and "Local and Regional Calls" sections in the front of the White Pages of the telephone directory. Familiarize yourself with your options and don't let the salesperson pressure or convince you to order "extra" services (e.g. call waiting, unlisted number, etc.) that you do not need. These extra features incur extra charges over and above the cost of basic service. Cell phone service may be considered as an alternative or an addition to your landline service.

Long Distance and International Service

You need to select a company to provide your international and U.S. long distance calls. There are a number of long distance companies; some of the most widely used are AT&T, MCI, and Sprint. Your local phone company may also offer long distance service.

Long distance providers offer a variety of services and pricing plans. Think about how often and at what times of day you will make long distance or international calls. Charges vary based on what time you make the call and where you are calling. You can call the long distance companies to get specific information about their costs, services and special low-cost calling plans for long distance and international calls. Remember, long distance service is considerably more expensive than local calls, so it pays to shop around for a cost-effective plan.

Pay Phones

There are many pay phones located around New York, though many are frequently out of service. You can use coins, calling cards (prepaid cards with an ID number that you enter to access your calling credit) or collect calling (where the person you are calling accepts the charges) to pay for your call. Local calls from pay phones on the street cost $0.50 (unlimited amount of time), or else $0.25 for 3 minutes, after which an automatic operator will ask you to deposit more change to continue your call. Dialing **911** for an emergency is always **free**.

Fax Machines

Fax machines enable you to send a printed document from telephone to telephone, or from modem to modem on personal computers. Even though fax machines have recently become more affordable, most students opt not to buy one for their home use; these machines are more commonly used in offices and businesses. Should you need to send or receive a fax, local stationery stores and copy/printing shops usually have machines that can be used by the public for approximately $1.00 to $3.00 per page for local faxes.

Mail

Post offices are located in all neighborhoods of New York City. To find a complete listing check the telephone book under "United States Postal Service." The postal service also has a website (**www.usps.com**) where you can find zip codes, locate post offices and view their hours of operation, buy stamps and calculate postage rates, and notify the post office if you change your address. Stamps may be purchased individually, in books of 10, or in rolls of 100.

You can get informational pamphlets listing domestic and international rates at your local post office free of charge. Try to buy your stamps at the post office in order to avoid the extra charges sometimes added by convenience stores or stamp machines. Stamped letters may be brought to the post office or dropped into any blue mailbox on the street.

Postage rates:*

DOMESTIC

Letters under 1 oz, first-class: $0.42
Postcards: $0.27

OVERSEAS

Letters under 1 oz, to Canada and Mexico: $0.72
Letters under 1 oz to all Other Countries: $0.94
Postcards to Canada and Mexico: $0.72
Postcards to all Other Countries: $0.94

*These prices were accurate at the time this book was published.

Mail is delivered once a day Monday through Saturday, usually between the hours of 10:00 a.m. and 3:00 p.m. Post office hours are different per location but generally are from 8:00 a.m. to 5:30 p.m., Monday through Friday, and until 4:00 p.m. on Saturday. They are closed on Sundays and on legal holidays. The General Post Office (Eighth Avenue and 33rd Street) and Grand Central Station (Lexington Avenue and 45th Street) have extended hours.

The standard way of addressing envelopes and packages in the U.S. is illustrated below. When sending mail to a U.S. address, be sure to include the apartment number, if known, and the zip code—a set of 5 to 9 digits that corresponds to a particular geographic area.

Jane Doe
1234 West 45th Street
New York, NY 10036

STAMP

One To World
285 West Broadway
New York, NY 10013

Special U.S. Postal Services

Mail can be sent "certified" or "registered" for an extra charge if you are sending something valuable—upon delivery the receiver must sign to accept the package or letter. If speed of delivery is urgent, you can send your package / letter through the post office's Express Mail, which provides overnight service in the U.S. and expedited delivery to foreign countries. Priority Mail takes one to three days in many areas and is slightly cheaper than Express Mail. If you need to send money, you can purchase a postal money order in either U.S. or foreign currency. You can also rent a Post Office Box (PO Box), if you move or travel frequently and want a safe place to collect your mail.

Private Delivery

There are many independent delivery companies, some of which offer greater convenience than the United States Post Office. Prices vary from company to company. Two of the more commonly used are United Parcel Service (UPS) and Federal Express (FedEx). Both deliver overnight within the U.S. and to many international destinations. For information on UPS, call (800) 742-5877 or go to **www.ups.com**. For Federal Express, call (800) 463-3339, go to **www.fedex.com**, or visit a packaging store.

SHOPPING

New York City is known worldwide as a shoppers' paradise. The key to ensuring that your New York City shopping experience lives up to its reputation is figuring out what you need to purchase and in what area you are likely to find it, and planning your shopping trip accordingly.

Buying Furniture & Housewares

If you plan to buy new furniture and housewares for your apartment, there are a number of reasonably priced stores—such as IKEA—that you can visit, either online or in person. Major department stores and retailers such as Bloomingdale's, Macy's, Century 21, Bed Bath and Beyond, Target, TJ Maxx, Home Goods and Kmart are good options to explore when setting up your new home. While higher-end stores such as Crate & Barrel, Pottery Barn, ABC Carpet & Home, Restoration Hardware and Williams Sonoma may not be in your budget, these stores sometimes offer good deals (and are great for "window" shopping!")

Alternatively, it is worth checking bulletin boards (on campus and around your neighborhood) for second-hand furnishings for sale and also notices of garage or stoop sales. Online bulletin boards such as Craigslist (**www.craigslist.com**) are good resources for affordable household items. Neighborhood thrift shops such as Housing Works, the Salvation Army and Goodwill, are also good options to explore when seeking low-cost, second-hand furnishing. In some areas, like the Upper East Side, you may even be lucky enough to find nice items that have been thrown out and left on the pavement for collection.

For necessities and small household items, it is often simpler and cheaper to stay in your neighborhood—look for dollar stores, discount stores, or branches of K-Mart, Duane Reade, Rite Aid, Target or CVS. One aspect of New York's distinct shopping culture are bodegas. These are independently owned neighborhood markets found on almost every corner. You can find food and drink staples here such as milk, coffee, candy, eggs, pasta, candy, and beer.

Department Stores

If you're looking for one-stop shopping and a taste of New York, visit one of the city's many department stores, where you can find an array of products for a variety of prices all under one roof. Known as "the largest department store in the world," **Macy's** (34th Street and Broadway) is a popular place to start. **Century 21** (22 Cortlandt Street, between Church and Broadway) is known as "New York's Best Kept Secret" and offers quality brand name items at a fraction of the cost at other major department stores. The well-known **Bloomingdale's** (59th Street and Lexington Avenue) is another option. Manhattan stores and the streets around them will be at their busiest on weekday lunchtimes, after working hours and on Saturdays. Weekday mornings usually offer the best chance of finding stores a little quieter.

A recent addition to Brooklyn is the large Swedish-based department store, **IKEA**. Located at **1 Beard Street in Red Hook**, this store is world-famous for its extensive and inexpensive selection of stylish furniture. It is accessible by the F, D, M, or R train at the 4th Ave / 9th St station or 2, 3, 4, 5, M, or R train to Court Street / Borough Hall. There are free shuttle buses directly to IKEA from either of these locations that leave every 15 minutes from 10 a.m. – 10 p.m. IKEA also offers a water taxi that departs about every 40 minutes from Pier 11 on the east side of the Financial District. The first taxi departs from Manhattan at 10 a.m. and the last taxi leaves IKEA at 9:40 p.m.

Most items purchased in New York City stores are subject to a sales tax of 8.625%. Groceries (food items) are not taxed, but food prepared in restaurants is taxed. Note that the prices marked on goods in stores are all pre-tax; once you make a purchase the tax is added. There are occasional "Tax Free Weeks" in New York during which no tax is levied on certain purchases of clothing or shoes. Smart shoppers sometimes choose to head to New Jersey where there is no sales tax on clothing!

Always ask for a receipt whenever you make a purchase, and find out about the store's refund and exchange policy. Should you need to return a purchase, make sure you show your original receipt and, if possible, keep all price tags intact. Most stores will refund your money in the form in which you paid, issue you a store credit, or allow you to exchange for another item in the store. If a store fails to honor its stated return policy, you can contact the **Better Business Bureau** at (212) 533-6200, the **New York City Department of Consumer Affairs** at 311, or the **New York State Consumer Protection Board**.

Food Shopping

You can do most of your food shopping at local supermarkets; small neighborhood grocery stores or delis generally charge higher prices. Associated Foods and Food Emporium are two large grocery stores in Manhattan that have numerous locations throughout the island. If you are looking for higher quality or all organic foods, Whole Foods is probably your best bet, though it can be rather expensive. For high quality without the high price, and a selection of $3 bottles of wine, try Trader Joe's at Union Square (14th Street and 3rd Avenue.) Another Trader Joe's is located in Cobble Hill (Court Street and Atlantic Avenue), but wine is not sold.

One way to save money on groceries is to use coupons, which you can find in newspapers or in supermarket circulars. You must present coupons to the cashier when you make your purchase. Note the expiration date, face value, and any restrictions before using them.

Farmers from nearby farms sell their fresh produce at outdoor markets (called "Greenmarkets") throughout the year; one of the largest is the market at Union Square (East 17th Street and Broadway). For information on Greenmarket locations and schedules, call the **Council on the Environment of New York City** at (212) 788-7900.

Another option is Fresh Direct, an online supermarket that delivers your groceries or meals to your door. This is a growing trend in New York City due to the ease and accessibility of the program, granted your apartment or house is in a deliverable area. Though it may seem like an expensive option, many find that many products are actually cheaper than in-store supermarkets. They usually have special discounts for new customers.

One of the best and environmentally friendly ways to save money on groceries and have access to some of the best quality produce in the city is to join a co-op (short for "cooperative"). A co-op is an organization composed of individual members who volunteer their time in exchange for discounted prices on a commodity (food, in this case). In this situation, you become a working member of a co-op that is supported and stocked by local farmers. In exchange for your work, usually 2 – 3 hours a month, you receive shopping access to the co-op store. Whereas most grocery stores mark up their prices by 100% by the time they reach the shelves, co-ops only mark up their prices between 20% – 40% on food items. There are many co-ops in Brooklyn especially, the Park Slope Co-op being the largest with almost 12,000 members.

Sales and Discounts

Sales are a blessing for the budget-conscious student. Department stores and boutiques offer sales at various times throughout the year. Usually the best time for bargains is during holidays (especially just after Christmas) and at the close of each season (for example, summer clothing goes on sale in July, and winter clothing in February). If you watch for sale announcements in newspaper or television advertisements, you can buy quality items at reduced prices. A great bargain shopping opportunity for the clothes shopper is the sample sale—a short sale during which a designer sells off samples of the upcoming season's collection or leftover stock, usually at reductions between 50% and 70%. For the serious "shopaholic," there are publications and websites that detail all upcoming sales and discount offers, such as the shopping section of **www.nymag.com**. Or check out these websites for more deals and savings: **http://nyc.urbansavings.com/** or **http://newyork.citylaunch.com/**.

You can also find inexpensive clothing and other items at street fairs, which are typically held on weekends during the summer, and at flea markets. Canal Street, in Chinatown, is a great place to find deals on small items such as costume jewelry, perfumes, and shoes. Prices at these street fairs and markets are often negotiable— don't be afraid to bargain! Go to **www.newyorkled.com** and click on "NEW YORK CITY Events" for street fair times and locations. For cheap furniture and household items, students often look for used or "second-hand" goods. Second-hand stores or "thrift stores" like **The Salvation Army** (use the "thrift store locator" to find a branch near you), **Goodwill** and **Housing Works** are smart places to start. Another resource is the popular website *Craigslist*. In the "For Sale" section of this site, New Yorkers who are moving house, leaving the city, or cleaning out their closets post ads to sell all kinds of items—there's even a "Free" category!

Flea markets and thrift stores have become especially popular in Brooklyn with the rise of a younger, predominantly college-age and young professional population. The Brooklyn Flea Market is held every Sunday during the summer and offers an extensive range of almost anything—furniture, vintage and new clothing, food, records, etc. Also in Brooklyn is Beacon's Closet, a veritable warehouse of hip consignment clothing at great prices in two locations: Park Slope and Williamsburg. As a side note, if you are looking to get rid of some old clothes and make some cash at the same time, many of these consignment stores also buy clothing. Be aware, however, that their standards are high in terms of season, trend, and brand when buying clothes from outside parties.

LIBRARIES

There are three separate public library systems in New York City: The New York Public Library System for Manhattan, the Bronx, and Staten Island; The Queens Borough Public Library System; and the Brooklyn Public Library System. The Mid-Manhattan Library (Fifth Avenue between 39th and 40th Sts.) is the central library of the New York system. There is also a library center in each borough: Donnell in Manhattan, Fordham in the Bronx, St. George on Staten Island, Central Library in Brooklyn, and Central Library in Queens. Aside from these, there are about 200 neighborhood branches throughout the five boroughs, including a branch for the visually impaired and physically disabled at 40 West 20th Street in Manhattan.

Library privileges are free and enable you to borrow books, films, CDs, cassettes and other materials from any branch in the system where you are registered. Proof of residency (such as a rent, telephone, or electric bill) is required in order to obtain a library card. Library materials can be borrowed at no cost for 1 – 3 weeks; however, an "overdue fee" is charged should you return an item later than the date it is due. For specific information on the New York Public Library, call their information number: (212) 930-0800/0830. Another valuable number is the Library's telephone Reference Service at (212) 340-0849, which will connect you to librarians who will try to answer any general interest or scholarly question you need researched.

Reference materials are available in every branch, but the most extensive collections are found at the five library centers and at the Mid-Manhattan Library. These materials must only be used in the library building; a photocopying service is provided. There are also four Research Libraries, with archives housing over 6 million volumes printed in more than 3,000 languages and dialects. These facilities are mainly designed for scholars, advanced students, and specialists conducting original research or intensive study. The Research Libraries include:

- Humanities and Social Sciences Library (Fifth Avenue and 42nd Street)
- Annex, The Research Libraries (521 West 43rd Street)
- Science, Industry and Business Library (188 Madison Avenue)
- New York Public Library for Performing Arts (40 Lincoln Center Plaza in Lincoln Center)
- Schomburg Center for Research in Black Culture (515 Lenox Avenue)

You can find a significant foreign language collection at the Donnell Library Center located at 20 West 53rd Street.

Expect banks, post offices, libraries, businesses, museums, most schools and some stores and restaurants to be closed on the following legal holidays:

January 1:	New Year's Day
3rd Monday in January:	Martin Luther King, Jr. Day
3rd Monday in February:	Presidents' Day
Last Monday in May:	Memorial Day
July 4:	Independence Day
1st Monday in September:	Labor Day
Second Monday in October:	Columbus Day
November 11:	Veterans Day
4th Thursday in November:	Thanksgiving Day
December 25:	Christmas Day

Religious holidays such as Passover, Easter, Ramadan, Yom Kippur, Rosh Hashanah, Hanukkah, and Kwanzaa are also observed by various communities in New York. The observance of one of your own religious holidays is always an acceptable excuse for absence from school or work but may require special communication with your professor or manager.

HINTS FOR HAVING FUN

What's Out There?

New York City is world renowned for its cultural and entertainment offerings. Virtually every type of event or activity you are interested in is offered somewhere in New York, and probably on a daily basis. On first arrival it can seem almost impossible to fully absorb and appreciate everything taking place throughout the city's five boroughs. The secret is to make yourself familiar with some of the publications and websites that exist to keep visitors and native city dwellers up-to-date on city happenings. Some of the most popular and useful are below. And keep your eyes and ears open for posters, fliers, and other announcements about gallery openings, concerts, poetry slams, and other activities!

Time Out **New York**

Self-titled the "obsessive guide to impulsive entertainment," this weekly magazine publishes near-exhaustive lists of museum and gallery exhibitions, comedy clubs, concerts and gigs, sporting events, shows and performances, along with reviews of restaurants, bars and cafes, and features on cultural events and New York life. *Time Out* can be purchased at newsstands and in bookstores (though if you are a regular reader it is much cheaper to get a subscription), or check out **www.timeout.com**.

Zagat Survey

This annually published book offers a comprehensive list of the city's restaurants and nightlife, along with reviews, recommendations and information on prices. *Zagats* is available in most bookstores, and online (for a fee) at **www.zagats.com**.

The Village Voice

The first and largest "alternative newsweekly," this free paper can be found in coffee shops, book stores and other locations throughout the city and includes an in-depth listing of New York City events. The *Voice* is also available online at **www.villagevoice.com**.

New York Magazine

Another weekly magazine offering up arts' entertainment, and nightlife listings, New York City restaurant guides and more, for sale at bookstores and newsstands. The popular online version of the magazine is available at www.newyorkmetro.com.

Not For Tourists Guide to New York

The black book of city guides. This compact book contains neighborhood and subway maps, listings for restaurants, shopping, nightlife, parks, events, community history, etc. It is a great resource to help the novice New Yorker to find their way around the city.

www.newyork.citysearch.com

This site serves as a virtual guide to the city, allowing you to access information on events, clubs, restaurants, hotels, shops, sports and favorite tourist attractions. Its search capabilities, weather updates, and maps make it a good all-around information site.

www.newyorkled.com

This site is popular with those looking to sample the city's cultural offerings without spending a fortune. It includes a daily events calendar and much more.

On a Budget

New York is an expensive city, but with a little ingenuity, you can enjoy it on a student budget. For just the price of a subway ride, you can explore the many unique, diverse neighborhoods that comprise the five boroughs. Hours can be spent strolling through Central Park, people-watching in Greenwich Village, or window-shopping on Fifth Avenue, all without spending a penny.

One place to start is **www.freenyc.net**. This website offers a listing of free events from music to sports to artistic happenings. It is a great resource for those who don't have money to burn or simply enjoy finding a deal.

Student rates are often available for museums, exhibitions, films and performances—be sure to ask when you purchase tickets and always carry your school ID. Most museums and cultural institutions also offer free entrance on certain days or during specific hours. For some museums, the admission price is always "suggested," rather than required. If you can't afford the suggested admission, you can pay a smaller amount or nothing at all and still enter the museum—keep in mind that many museums rely heavily on donations, so whatever you can offer will make a difference. For a listing of free museums, go to **www.ny.com/museums/free.html**.

Colleges and universities often sponsor special concerts, films, dances and other social activities. These are usually far less expensive than those offered by commercial groups, and attending these campus events can be a great way to meet other students.

Summertime transforms New York into a playground of free cultural activities, making it one of the best times to be a student in the city. Central Park offers free performances of Shakespeare (**www.publictheater.org** and **www.newyorkclassical.org**), the Metropolitan Opera (**www.metopera.org/parks**), and popular singers and bands on their specially constructed "Summerstage" (**www.summerstage.org**). Summer celebrations like Harlem Week and Gay Pride offer scores of free events. Street festivals and parades take over areas of the city weekend after weekend, and it's hard to turn a corner without stumbling on a free outdoor film screening or concert.

Nightlife

New York, "the city that never sleeps," can be even more exciting at night than during the day. The streets in some neighborhoods, such as the East and West Villages and SoHo, are just as crowded at 2 a.m. as they are at 2 p.m.! The variety of nightclubs, bars, and discotheques is astounding—unfortunately, sometimes the costs are, too. Many clubs, especially those offering live music, may have a "cover charge" (an admission fee) and/or a "drink minimum" which obligates you to buy at least one or two drinks. Cover charges are usually lower on weekdays than on weekends.

Remember, you must be at least 21 years of age in order to purchase or be served alcoholic beverages. Expect to be asked to show identification before entering a bar or club, when buying an alcoholic drink, and when buying alcohol at a store. Acceptable IDs will have your photo and your date of birth. A driver's license or passport is the most commonly accepted form of identification. You must be at least 18 years of age to purchase cigarettes, and may be asked to show ID to do so.

STAYING HEALTHY

Coping With Culture Shock

Like all college students, you will need a few months to acclimate to your new surroundings. As an international student, moreover, you will probably experience a form of "culture shock" when you suddenly find yourself immersed in a new environment, with a different schedule, different customs, and different foods than you are used to. Moving overseas can produce feelings of disorientation and transition to varying degrees in almost everyone. It can be difficult to move from a familiar setting where you may have many friends and family to a large city such as New York, which is busy, fast-paced, and at times impersonal. During the first few months if you feel isolated, "different" or as though you don't "fit in," don't worry—this is a completely normal reaction which will pass as you adjust to living in a new country. It is important to be able to communicate the way you're feeling: talk to your international student advisor or college mentor, or get involved with other international students who will probably have experienced similar feelings at some stage. **One To World runs many programs that bring international students together in various ways**—why not join a One To World program and make friends with others who understand how you are feeling!

At times the stress of a new environment may also take a toll on your body. It is extremely important to eat well (limit your intake of fatty fast foods and be sure to add fresh fruits and vegetables to your daily diet), exercise, and sleep for a reasonable number of hours per night. You should also know how to seek help in the event that you require medical attention.

Medical Insurance

Medical service in the United States is not nationalized and is therefore very expensive. Many U.S. residents participate in private health insurance plans that cover their hospital, doctor, and dentist fees up to a specified maximum cost. The terms of your U.S. visa require that you and any accompanying family members are adequately covered by health insurance. Most academic institutions have either a compulsory or an optional insurance plan, with coverage available for their students' families at an additional cost. See your International Student Advisor for policy information and referrals to appropriate insurance companies.

Once you are enrolled with a health insurance provider, you will receive a card with an ID number from them. You should carry this with you all times in case of an emergency.

Physicians

Many universities and colleges have a campus health service with nurses and doctors who provide medical treatment for free or for a reduced fee. Often these centers treat only general, common complaints such as colds or the flu, but if you do require specialized attention, they are prepared to refer you to an outside specialist. It's always a good idea to consult your campus health service first before deciding whether or not to see a physician outside of school, which can cost several hundred dollars.

If you do choose to use a non-campus health service physician, it makes sense to establish contact before you become ill so that you will know where to turn when you have a medical problem. To find a personal physician, ask for referrals from people you know or your school's health service. Other options include contacting the hospital in your neighborhood or your local county medical society. Physicians' schedules are often full and they may only accept appointments for two or three weeks in advance. If you are sick and need an appointment right away, you should make this clear when you call and be firm about your urgent need to see the doctor.

Hospitals

All New York City hospitals, both private and public (city- and / or state-operated), offer short-term, long-term, and emergency treatment.

"Out-Patient" clinics provide short-term care. These clinics provide services similar to those of private doctors when you are ill but do not need to stay in the hospital. They are usually staffed by interns and residents (doctors who have recently completed medical school and are pursuing further training) who are supervised by more senior attending physicians. As a rule, there can be a long wait before you get to see a medical attendant in an out-patient clinic, but these clinics often provide access to specialists who would be much more expensive if seen privately. This is particularly true in teaching hospitals (those affiliated with medical schools).

"In-Patient" treatment is the longer-term care that you receive when you are admitted into the hospital. The hospital where you are treated is determined by your doctor's hospital affiliation; every doctor is required to affiliate with a specific hospital in order to be able to admit patients.

If you have a serious emergency and do not know a doctor, go to the emergency room of the nearest hospital. Emergency rooms are open 24 hours a day, seven days a week. If you are too ill to get to the hospital, call an ambulance by dialing 911 on the telephone (but note that there will be a substantial charge for ambulance service if this is not covered by your health insurance). Emergency rooms always give priority to the most seriously ill patients, so if your problem is not life-threatening, you can expect to wait a long time before you receive treatment.

Dental Care

Like physicians, dentists with private practices can be expensive. The health service at your school may be able to recommend a dentist in your neighborhood. Both Columbia and New York University offer dental clinics that are open to the general public for fees that are much lower than those charged by private dentists. The work is performed by students under the careful supervision of trained dentists. Call for hours and appointments:

Columbia University School of Dental and Oral Surgery
Information on all six Columbia University dental locations:
http://dental.columbia.edu/patients/index

Dental Center of New York University
345 East 24th Street
New York, NY 10010
(212) 998-9872
www.nyu.edu/dental/patientinfo/index.html

If you are unable to reach your dentist and require immediate attention, call the Emergency Dental Service at (212) 573-9502, for referral to a dentist in your area who can see you right away.

Pharmacies

Medication that has been prescribed by your physician can be purchased at a pharmacy or drugstore. You must present the slip of paper on which your doctor has written your prescription and wait (usually 15 – 60 minutes) to obtain your medication. Pharmacists are medical professionals and can answer many questions about the medication you have been prescribed. Check out the pharmacies in your area to find one that is convenient and that accepts your medical insurance. Several drugstores are open 24 hours a day, seven days a week.

Mental Health Care

It is not uncommon for college students to undergo periods of stress related to schoolwork, career decisions, and personal or social issues. Should anxieties or negative feelings persist or begin to interfere with your everyday well-being, you may wish to discuss them with a therapist. Try to remember that feeling under stress or unable to cope, or suffering from a condition such as depression, is not embarrassing or something to be ashamed of. Most likely your university health service has a confidential mental health/counseling division that is free of charge or partially subsidized for a limited number of visits. If you feel more comfortable seeking independent help, your campus health service should be able to make a confidential referral to a reliable counselor. Otherwise you may contact the Mental Health and Substance Abuse Referral Service at (800) 543-3638 (available 24 hours a day, seven days a week).

Women's Health Care

New York City offers a full range of health service for women. For general information and specific doctor referrals, call 311 and ask for Women's Health services. Planned Parenthood clinics offer reliable and inexpensive gynecological services, including birth control. For an appointment or information call (212) 965-7000 or (800) 230-PLAN, or go to **www.plannedparenthood.org/nyc/**.

In addition to these services, there are many toll-free crisis "hotline" telephone numbers you can call in the event of a mental health emergency. Hotline calls are handled confidentially by counselors trained in specific issues.

Some hotline numbers to make note of:

NYS HIV/AIDS Counseling Hotline	(800) 872-2777
Alcoholics Anonymous	(212) 870-3400
Narcotics Anonymous	(212) 929-6262
Rape Hotline	(212) 267-7273
Suicide Prevention Line	(800) 784-2433
Gay Men's Health Crisis AIDS Hotline	(212) 807-6655
Alcohol & Substance Abuse Information	(800) 522-5353 (8 a.m. – 10 p.m.)

BRINGING YOUR FAMILY

If you are married, you may be thinking about having your spouse and/or your children accompany you to the U.S. for all or part of your academic program. This is a big decision, which each family ultimately needs to weigh based on its individual circumstances. Here are some of the issues you might want to consider.

On the positive side, the opportunity to immerse oneself in a foreign culture can be a life-enriching experience, and you may be looking forward to sharing this experience with your spouse and children for a period of time. Exposure to an English-speaking environment—especially for children—can greatly facilitate the learning of English and provide a lifelong benefit for each member of your family. As an international student or scholar far from home, moreover, you may find that having your family with you in the U.S. provides you with a source of emotional support and enables you to avoid the anxiety of a long separation or of worrying about how they are doing at home without you.

On the other hand, bringing your family to the U.S. can add considerably to the cost of your stay, at a time when your budget may already be tight. You will need to provide proof that you have sufficient funds to support your family members in the U.S. before being able to secure visas for them. You can expect your expenses to be significantly higher, especially for housing, food, and health insurance. Since it may be impossible for your spouse to work, you may not be able to count on supplementary income that you may be accustomed to at home. Finally, the presence of family members dealing with their own adjustment issues can sometimes pose difficult demands on your time or attention and possibly distract you from your primary goal of completing your degree program or research project.

Here are some things to think about as you plan whether or not to bring your family with you.

Family Housing

International students and scholars report that finding suitable and affordable housing is one of the biggest obstacles to having their families with them in the New York area. It's a good idea to have your spouse and/or children delay their arrival until you have arranged a place for your family to live. This is especially important if you have school-age children whom you want to enroll in public school, since the school they attend will depend upon where you reside.

Check with your academic institution to see if married student housing is available. The off-campus student housing office is another good source of options for apartments suitable for families. Faculty in your department may know of available housing; let all your local friends and any relatives know that you are looking. Be sure to consult the housing section of this book.

Childcare

Children under the age of four or five are not eligible for public school, so if you and/ or your spouse are unable to care for them at all times, you will need to explore other childcare options. Young children should never be left alone; parents who do so may be subject to legal action. Unless you are lucky enough to have relatives in the NY area, the extended family that may help with childcare in your home country will not be available, and there are no government-provided nursery or daycare facilities.

Childcare options include daycare centers and private nursery schools, where you pay to enroll your child in a program, and private babysitters, who may care for one or several children simultaneously, either in their own homes or in your home. The student employment office on your campus is a good place to look for students who are available to work as babysitters for an hourly wage. Before hiring any childcare provider, you should always ask for references and arrange to speak with parents for whom the person has previously worked. For daycare centers, a good place to begin your research is online at **www.naeyc.org/accreditation/center_search.asp**.

Schooling For Your Children

By law in New York, any child between the ages of 5 and 21 who has not already received a high school diploma is entitled to attend public school free of charge. In New York City, your child may start public school in September of the year that he or she turns five. In some areas, there are public pre-kindergarten ("pre-K") programs available for 4-year olds, but places may be limited and are not guaranteed.

The New York City public school system is large and complex; it serves over 1 million students and includes 1,200 schools. The public school your child may attend usually depends upon the "zone" in which you are living. Official information on finding your zoned school and learning about other options can be found on the website of the New York City Department of Education; see **http://schools.nyc.gov/default.aspx**. See also "A Guide for Parents and Families" **http://schools.nyc.gov/ParentsFamilies/NYCFamilyGuide.htm**.

Here are some other useful websites:
http://home.earthlink.net/~schoolsandyou/textdocs/resources.html
www.insideschools.org

If you plan to enroll your child in public school, you will need to present a copy of the child's birth certificate and proof of required immunizations. The school year begins in early September and ends in mid- to late-June.

Private (independent) and parochial (Catholic) schools are also available throughout the New York area. Students must go through an application and testing process, and tuition can be quite expensive. For information on these options, see **www.nais.org/admission/schoolSearch.cfm** (for independent schools) and **www.archny.org/school-search/** (for Catholic schools).

Activities For Your Spouse

It's a good idea to do some advance thinking about how your spouse will spend his / her time in the U.S. If your spouse is not as fluent in English as you are, be prepared for the language barrier to pose a handicap, at least initially. If your spouse is employed or has a professional career in your home country, he or she will need to prepare for the potential frustration of not being eligible to work in the U.S. (Spouses of students on F-1 visas are not allowed to work; spouses of J-1 students/scholars may work only under specific circumstances. Consult the International Student Advisor on your campus.)

Fortunately, the New York City area provides an abundance of resources to help support international spouses. Begin with the International Student Office at your institution and see what special programs or services they may offer. These may include regular spouse club meetings, free or low-cost English language lessons, and other activities.

Another excellent volunteer opportunity is One To World's *Global Classroom* program through which international students / scholars and spouses can visit New York City schools and make presentations on their home countries and cultures. For additional ideas for your spouse, see the section on "Resources for International Students" in the appendix.

FINANCIAL AID FOR INTERNATIONAL STUDENTS

For foreign nationals, financial assistance to study in the United States—grants, scholarships, fellowships and teaching assistantships—is very limited, especially at the undergraduate level. Applying for financial assistance requires considerable research and lead time. You should be aware that most financial aid is awarded on a competitive basis, and that application deadlines are often a full year or more prior to the award date.

Sources of funds for study in the U.S. include academic institutions, private foundations, U.S. government and foreign governments, corporations, research institutes, and bi-national agencies. If you are seeking financial aid for U.S. study, your first task will be to research available sources of funding and identify those for which you believe you are eligible to apply. Libraries and educational advising centers in your home country (contact the U.S. Embassy to locate the nearest U.S. educational advising center) are good places to start your research. The U.S. Embassy can also give you information about how to apply for a Fulbright scholarship for graduate study in the U.S.

If a university in your home country operates a direct exchange program with a U.S. institution, find out if you are eligible to participate and receive financial aid. You should also look into opportunities offered by your own government or private organizations in your home country.

In the New York area, the Institute of International Education's Information Center provides extensive information resources for foreign nationals interested in studying, teaching, interning, or volunteering in the U.S. You will want to consult the IIE publication called *Funding for U.S. Study: A Guide for International Students and Professionals*, as well as other reference books and handouts available at the center.

Institute of International Education (IIE) Information Center
809 United Nations Plaza (between 45th & 46th Streets)
New York, NY 10017
www.iie.org

If you are already in the U.S., be sure to consult with your school's Financial Aid Office, International Student Office, the Career Planning and Placement Office, and/ or individual academic departments to find out what financial resources are available to foreign nationals and how to go about applying for them.

The Internet is another excellent source of information for researching financial assistance for study in the United States. Here are some websites to get you started:

- www.edupass.org
- http://fdncenter.org
- www.princetonreview.com;
- www.fastaid.com
- www.iefa.org
- www.college.ucla.edu/up/src/international/intl.htm

(Please note: Following is an overview of issues foreigners living temporarily in the U.S. should be aware of regarding your obligations as a temporary resident of the U.S. This information is particularly directed towards international students and exchange visitors; it should not be viewed as individual legal advice. Immigration laws are highly complex and technical; any legal issues should be reviewed with a qualified immigration attorney.)

Immigration Issues

As with any country in the world, the United States has laws and regulations governing foreigners living temporarily within its boundaries. These regulations may sometimes seem confusing. If you are an international student or exchange visitor, your school's International Student Advisor (ISA) can help you understand these regulations, so that you can fulfill your legal obligations and maintain legal "nonimmigrant" status while in the U.S. Be aware that failure to maintain legal nonimmigrant status may have serious and unfavorable consequences. The following is a summary of essential responsibilities that you, as a nonimmigrant student, scholar, or exchange visitor, are responsible for carrying out with respect to U.S. immigration laws and regulations:

- Always keep your passport valid for at least six months in the future.
- Keep your Certificate of Eligibility (Form I-20 or DS-2019) valid at all times.
- If you are a student, maintain **full-time enrollment** during the academic year.
- Apply for any necessary extensions of stay at least 30–60 days **before** your present Certificate of Eligibility (Form I-20 or DS-2019) expires.
- Do **not** begin **any** type of employment (on-or-off campus) without consulting with your International Student Advisor. (**Note:** Most authorized employment on-or-off campus is limited to 20 hours per week while school is in session.)
- Do **not** engage in off-campus employment without first obtaining appropriate work authorization from the United States Citizenship and Immigration Service (USCIS). Your International Student Advisor can offer advice on how to apply for the necessary authorization.
- Do **not** travel outside the U.S., even briefly, without asking your International Student Advisor to sign your Certificate of Eligibility (Form I-20 or DS-2019). Your ISA will also be able to advise you on other documents you will need to take with you in order to leave and re-enter the U.S. with ease.
- Complete all required income tax forms and pay taxes when they are due. (**Note:** All international students—whether they have earned money or not—are required to file income tax forms.)
- Give truthful answers to any questions asked on immigration forms or by an immigration official.
- Always notify your International Student Advisor and obtain any necessary authorizations before changing your program of study or immigration status, and / or transferring to another academic institution.

- Do **not** rely on immigration-related advice from newspapers, friends, web pages, or "chat corners". Always consult your International Student Advisor *first*. If your International Student Advisor is unable to help you, s / he will refer you to an appropriate resource.
- Immediately upon your initial arrival on campus, have your International Student Advisor check your travel documents. Immigration inspectors sometimes make mistakes and it is best to correct them as soon as possible. Your advisor can help you correct an error.
- If you move your place of residence, inform your International Student Office and the campus Registrar's Office of your new address and telephone number within 10 days of the change.

There are serious consequences for nonimmigrants that violate immigration rules even in minor ways, particularly for those who stay in the U.S. beyond the authorized period of stay. These consequences include being barred from re-entering the United States for up to 10 years. It is very important that you are careful to maintain your status.

Your International Student Advisor is an important source of information and guidance during your academic career in the U.S. **Remember: immigration rules and regulations are complex and change frequently. Consult with your International Student Advisor on a regular basis, especially when you have any questions.**

Adjudication of U.S. immigration laws and regulations is the responsibility of **United States Citizenship and Immigration Services (USCIS)**. USCIS is a part of the U.S. Department of Homeland Security (DHS), whose headquarters are located in Washington, D.C. Two other important DHS branches are Immigration and Customs Enforcement (ICE), which oversees the Student and Exchange Visitor Program (SEVP) responsible for monitoring international student and scholar records and issues, and is responsible for the oversight of other investigatory functions. The other DHS branch is the U.S. Customs and Border Protection (CBP), whose officers inspect anyone seeking to enter, pass through, or remain in the U.S. Most transactions with DHS occur electronically or by mail, and usually the only DHS officials with whom you ever come into contact are the CBP officers at U.S. ports of entry when you travel.

Basic Travel Documents

If you plan to travel outside the United States, you should consult with your International Student Advisor first in order to make sure your travel documents are valid and in order. (Reminder: Make photocopies of all your travel documents and keep them in a safe place!) You will need to carry the following documents in order to exit and re-enter the United States:

- Passport valid for **at least** the next six months
- Valid Form I-20 or DS-2019 with the current endorsement by your International Student Advisor
- Valid U.S. Visa
- I-94 card obtained from airline or at border crossing
- Proof of financial support
- Evidence of employment authorization, if appropriate

When you arrive at your U.S. "port of entry," the immigration inspector will examine these travel documents and determine whether you can be admitted into the U.S.

Passport

You should always keep your passport valid for a minimum of six months into the future. Consult your country's consulate or embassy in the U.S. to renew your passport well in advance of the expiration date. Consulate officials will tell you what forms and fees, if any, are required for renewal. If you are required to supply a letter affirming that you are a matriculated, full-time student, you can request such a letter from your campus Registrar's Office.

Certificate of Eligibility (Form I-20 or DS-2019)

This basic travel document is issued by the academic institution which you will attend. The form I-20 or DS-2019 describes: 1) your school's name, your degree level, and your field of study; 2) your program's start date and expected date of completion; and 3) the means by which you will finance your U.S. study. This document also establishes your eligibility for such things as employment benefits and re-entry permission after travel abroad. If any of the information on this form changes (for instance, you decide to pursue a new degree program or field of study), you must apply to the International Student Advisor for a new Certificate of Eligibility. If you wish to transfer to a new school, you must instruct your current International Student Advisor to release your immigration record to your new school and then obtain an I-20 or DS-2019 from the new school. The I-20 or DS-2019 must always reflect what you are doing now.

All I-20 and DS-2019 forms are created in a DHS database called the Student and Exchange Visitor Information System (SEVIS). Your school has entered your biographical information, as well as information about your academic program and financial resources into SEVIS, and continuously updates your record to account for any changes (e.g. your local address, semester enrollments, and special authorizations such as for employment). Your I-20 or DS-2019 form contains a unique SEVIS number (starting with N and found in the upper right corner) that stays the same as long as you maintain continuously valid F-1 or J-1 immigration status.

You need to keep your form I-20 or DS-2019 in a safe place with your passport and I-94 card. If you travel outside the U.S., your International Student Advisor **must** sign the back of your form I-20 or DS-2019 before you leave the U.S. in order to certify that you are enrolled and otherwise eligible for re-entry in the same status. Be sure to pack your form I-20 or DS-2019 in your carry-on bag along with your passport and any other documents you may need to show to an immigration inspector.

Visa
A visa, the sticker placed inside your passport by the U.S. consul abroad, is needed to enter the U.S. Your visa shows the latest date on which you can apply to enter this country and the type of visa you have been granted (usually F-1 or J-1 for students or scholars), letting U.S. immigration officials know the type of activity you intend to engage in while in the country.

Should you need to renew your visa in order to re-enter the U.S., you will need to visit the U.S. consulate in your home country or in another country to which you are traveling before attempting to re-enter the U.S. If you are not a resident of the country to which you are traveling, first check with the country's U.S. consulate to make sure that they will accept your visa application for processing. **It is not possible to renew an F-1 or J-1 visa while you are within the borders of the U.S. (Note:** Don't worry if your visa expires while you are in the U.S., as long as your passport, Certificate of Eligibility, and I-94 card are still valid.) The purpose of the visa is to enter the U.S. These other documents control your stay. Visit your International Student Advisor well before you leave the U.S. to make certain your travel documents are in order.

Note: If you are traveling somewhere other than your home country, you may need an entry visa for that country; consult that country's embassy or consulate for information.

Form I-94

The I-94 card, issued to you upon arrival, shows that you have been lawfully admitted to the U.S. and is usually stapled across from the U.S. visa in your passport. It contains an eleven-digit admission number used by DHS to keep track of your arrival and departure from the U.S. The I-94 should be collected each time you depart from the U.S. and a new one issued upon re-entry, except in certain cases of trips of thirty days or less to Canada, Mexico, or the Caribbean.

I-94 cards issued to F-1 and J-1 visa holders usually do not indicate a fixed expiration date; rather, these I-94 cards simply show that the bearer may remain in the U.S. for the "Duration of Status" (D/S). This means that the individual is authorized to remain in the U.S. while pursuing the program of study described on his or her current I-20 or DS-2019. Students with I-94 cards marked "D/S" need to obtain permission to extend their stay if their I-20 or DS-2019 form is about to expire. Such extensions need to be authorized by your academic advisor and processed by your International Student Advisor well before your current program's end date. However, if you have an I-94 card with a specific expiration date, you must either leave the U.S. before that date or apply to USCIS for an extension of stay before the card expires. Procedures for extending your stay vary according to visa type. Consult your International Student Advisor for specific instructions.

Proof of Financial Support

Proof of financial support for your studies can be 1) a letter from a bank indicating the current balance in your bank account or in the account of your sponsor, as well as the average balance in the account during the previous year, 2) a completed affidavit of support (USCIS Form I-134) from your sponsor, including a notarized copy of his/her most recent U.S. or local income tax return and an employment letter if appropriate, or 3) a letter from a sponsoring agency outlining details of their financial award to you. Evidence of U.S. dollar equivalent alone should also be shown. If you are receiving any university funding, you should carry a letter outlining this support. Also, if you have an on-campus job, you should carry a letter from your employer stating the period of employment, your weekly hours (20 or less during the academic year) and your rate of pay. Be sure to at least have copies of these financial documents with you when attempting to enter the U.S.

Taxes

All international students and scholars must comply with U.S. federal, state, and local tax laws. This means that you **must** file tax forms every year **whether or not you have earned any money in the U.S.** Federal and state tax forms and instructions for filing may be obtained from your International Student Office on campus or directly from the Internal Revenue Service (IRS) and state tax offices and their corresponding websites.

In the United States, there are three types of income tax: federal, state, and Social Security / Medicare (also called "FICA," Federal Insurance Contribution Act). These three taxes are also referred to as "withholdings" because at each pay period, a certain amount of tax is withheld (deducted) from workers' paychecks for tax purposes. International students are usually exempt from FICA or Social Security / Medicare withholdings during their first five years in the U.S., but after this period most are required to begin paying into the Social Security system. If you are exempt from FICA, make sure that your employer does not withhold Social Security / Medicare (FICA) tax from your pay or stipend checks by checking your pay stubs. There may also be state and individual taxes.

Social Security Number (SSN) and Individual Taxpayer Identification Number (ITIN)

If you are employed in the U.S. or receive a stipend from your school, you are **required** to have a **Social Security Number (SSN)**. The number is required for IRS reporting purposes. Your International Student Advisor can assist you in obtaining a Social Security Number.

Students who are ineligible for a Social Security Number may be required to obtain an IRS Individual **Taxpayer Identification Number (ITIN)**. The ITIN is a nine-digit number issued by the IRS for tax filing use only. Your International Student Advisor can assist you in filing for an ITIN.

To obtain appropriate tax forms and publications, you may contact the IRS directly:
IRS Information: (800) 829-1040
IRS Tax Forms and Publications Division: (800) 829-3676
www.irs.gov

For information about New York State taxes, contact:
The New York State Department of Taxation and Finance
Personal Income Tax Information Center: (800) 443-3200
www.tax.state.ny.us

For information about New Jersey State taxes, contact:
The Jersey Department of Taxation and Finance
Taxpayer Customer Service Center: (609) 292-6400
www.state.nj.us/treasury/taxation/

Some Useful Websites
U.S. Citizenship and Immigration Services: **http://uscis.gov/graphics/index.htm**
U.S. Department of State: **http://exchanges.state.gov/jexchanges/index.html**
Social Security Administration: **www.ssa.gov**

GETTING READY TO LEAVE NEW YORK

As your time studying or working in New York draws to a close, there will be many different things for you to think about. It can be all too easy to get caught up in preparations for your departure and forget that there are bills you need to pay and requirements you still need to fulfill for your college or institution. The following list should serve as a guide to some essential things that you need to do before you leave the city or the country.

- If you have rented your own apartment, be sure to notify your landlord in writing at least a month before your departure date. Avoid losing your security deposit or being charged extra fees by fulfilling all the terms of your lease.

- Notify your telephone, electricity and cable TV suppliers of the date on which they should terminate service. Arrange for refunds of any deposits you may have paid.

- Notify the post office of your date of departure and provide your forwarding address. Ask the post office for special change-of-address postcards you can send to any companies with which you maintain magazine or newspaper subscriptions.

- Leave your forwarding address with the International Student Office and the registrar at your university.

- Be sure to pay all outstanding bills, including credit cards, library fees, and any university fees.

- Make sure you obtain an official copy of your college transcript.

- Return all materials you have borrowed from libraries.

- Let your international student advisor know that you are leaving the country and find out what procedures you may need to go through before, during, or after your departure.

- Consider donating any clothing or household items you are unable to take home with you to local charities, such as The Salvation Army.

It is also important to consider that you may feel some effects of "reverse" culture shock as you re-enter life in your home country. After making a new life here in New York, it can seem strange to be back at home among old surroundings and people who haven't had the transformational experiences you have. You may start to realize how much you have changed and to feel that you no longer fit into exactly the same place as you did before you went away. A readjustment period after returning home is inevitable, but if you are prepared for it, it should be easier for you to cope with life after New York!

RESOURCES FOR INTERNATIONAL STUDENTS

International Student Service Organizations

The organizations described below offer a variety of programs, activities, services and publications especially for the international student community. International student associations, national clubs, and many campus-based organizations also sponsor film festivals, concerts, sporting events and social activities throughout the year. Your school's International Student Office is a good source of information on activities that are open to you. You should also make a note of the following nonprofit organizations that can help you make the most of your time in the New York City area.

One To World

285 West Broadway, Suite #450
New York, NY 10013
Tel: (212) 431-1195
info@one-to-world.org
www.one-to-world.org

One To World should be your first stop for finding out how to discover New York and meet Americans! We offer special events for international students and scholars throughout the academic year: community visits with American host families, walking tours, foreign affairs conferences, social activities for international spouses, and much more. You can also join our Global Classroom program and go into New York City schools to make presentations on your home country and culture. Contact us for more information and to put your name on our mailing list.

Institute of International Education (IIE)

Information Center
809 United Nations Plaza
New York, NY 10017
Tel: (212) 984-5400
www.iie.org

The Information Center at IIE provides a wealth of resources for people doing research on study abroad or study in the United States. Visitors can use their extensive collection of university catalogues and information files. Information about internships, volunteerism, transferring to another school, and financial aid (scholarships, grants and fellowships) is also available. Volunteers at the center assist visitors with research inquiries. No membership fee is required. The Information Center is open to the public on Tuesday, Wednesday & Thursday, 11:00 a.m. – 3:45 p.m. except major holidays. (Note: The Information Center is a walk-in center only. They do not respond to telephone or mail inquiries.)

International Center in New York

50 West 23rd Street, 7th Floor
New York, NY 10010-5205
Tel: (212) 255-9555
icny@intlcenter.org
www.intlcenter.org

Open Monday through Friday 10 a.m. – 8 p.m. and Saturday 9:30 a.m. – 3:30 p.m., the International Center serves foreign students, exchange scholars and other internationals. Services include individual English lessons, social and cultural activities, invitations to American homes, tickets to N.Y. theatre and concert programs, as well as advice about finding jobs and housing. Programs are run by American volunteers. The annual registration fee is $350.00 ($300 for six months). An optional twelve hours of one-to-one English language tutoring is also available for an additional $80.00.

International House
500 Riverside Drive
New York, NY 10027
Tel: (212) 316-8400
www.ihouse-New York City.org
International House is a residence and
program center for 700 graduate students,
interns and trainees from over 100 countries.
Activities include guest speakers, seminars,
films, trips, festivals, music recitals and social
events. Facilities include study rooms and
music practice rooms, and a cafeteria, pub,
fitness center, and gymnasium. Scholarships
are available for residents. Non-resident
memberships are available to full-time
graduate students, interns and trainees of
21 years and older for $150.00 per year or $75
per semester. For information on non-resident
memberships call (212) 316-8436.

YMCA International
5 West 63rd Street, 2nd Floor
New York, NY 10023
Tel: (212) 727-8800
Toll Free: (888) 477-9622
ips@ymcaNew York City.org
www.ymcainternational.org
The International Branch of the YMCA
sponsors inexpensive educational travel
programs to different areas of interest in the
U.S. These usually happen in the summer and
can be arranged from your home country.
Their office is open from Monday to Friday
9 a.m. – 5 p.m., and they can provide you with
a listing of Y hostels in the U.S. and abroad for
student travelers. Their International Career
Advancement Program helps trainees to
find a host site in the U.S. and arranges their
visas. Check www.ymcaicap.org for more
information.

English Conversation Programs

Most colleges and universities in New York
have English Conversation Programs on
campus. If you would like to find a program
outside your school, the organizations
listed below offer one-to-one English
conversation practice. Registration fees
and tutoring hours vary from program to
program. Call for specific information.

International Center in New York
50 West 23rd Street, 7th Floor
New York, NY 10010-5205
Tel: (212) 255-9555
icny@mindspring.com
www.intlcenter.org

English-Speaking Union of the United States
144 East 39th Street
New York, NY 10016
Tel: (212) 818-1200
info@esuus.org
http://www.esuus.org
Ask about "English in Action"

Riverside Church
490 Riverside Drive
New York, NY 10027
Tel: (212) 870-6735
English Conversation Program offered
September – May

Volunteering

Donating your time and talent can be a
great way to meet people, learn more
about your new community and American
life, and give something back. Volunteer
opportunities abound in New York City—
the websites below can help you figure out
what kind of volunteer work you'd like to do
and where to find it.

www.one-to-world.org
Consider volunteering at the One To World
office or through our community service
programs. Through the *Global Classroom*
program, you get the opportunity to go into
New York City public school classrooms to
teach K-12 students about your country and
culture.

www.volunteermatch.org
Search for long-term or event based volunteer
opportunities available in your area from a
wide array of organizations.

www.idealist.org
Listings of volunteer positions with NGO's
and other not-for-profit organizations in your
community and around the world, and in a
variety of fields. Sign up to receive personal
email updates matching your volunteer
interests.

www.nycares.org

Offers hands-on, team-based and flexible volunteer projects in New York City. Volunteer fields include work with the homeless, children, fighting hunger, urban renewal and the environment.

Lesbian, Gay, Bisexual and Transgender (LGBT) Services

The following list of resources can help you get involved in the LGBT community, find health and support services and learn about special opportunities for LGBT students. Your school may also have an LGBT office or student group, or offer LGBT services - ask your International Student Advisor for information.

Lesbian, Gay, Bisexual and Transgender Community Center

208 West 13th Street
New York, NY 10011
Tel: (212) 620-7310
www.gaycenter.org

Comprehensive and up-to-date information on events, group meetings, educational programs and other resources sponsored by this center.

The Audre Lorde Project

85 South Oxford Street
Brooklyn, NY 11217-1607
Tel: (718) 596-0342
www.alp.org/index.html

New York's center for lesbians, gays, bisexuals and transgender people of color.

Callen-Lorde Community Health Center

356 West 18th Street
New York, NY 10011
Tel: (212) 271-7200
www.callen-lorde.org/index.html

New York's only medical facility dedicated to meeting the health care needs of the LGBT communities and people living with HIV / AIDS—regardless of any patient's ability to pay.

LGBT Student Scholarships
www.american.edu/ocl/glbta/resources/ info_scholarships.html

List of scholarships available specifically for LGBT Students, compiled by the American University Office of Financial Aid.

Gay and Lesbian National Hotline
Toll Free: (888) 843-4564
www.glnh.org

The Gay & Lesbian National Hotline offers free and anonymous counseling services over a toll-free telephone number. Callers can speak directly with a trained volunteer who has access to a national database of referrals specific to the gay and lesbian community. GLNH is open Monday through Friday, 4 p.m. – midnight and Saturday noon – 5 p.m. EST.

Students with Disabilities

An array of services and organizations exist to serve people with disabilities in New York City. The resources below can help you figure out how to navigate the city and to find support. Contact your International Student Advisor to learn more about your school's services and offerings for disabled students.

The Mayor's Office for People with Disabilities

100 Gold Street
2nd Floor
New York, NY 10038
Tel: (212) 788-2830
www.New York City.gov/html/mopd/

Offers information on community resources and city resources accessible to people with disabilities and publishes *Access New York: A Guide to Accessible Travel In and Around New York City*, This is a free practical guide with detailed information about transport, dining out, attractions, museums, theaters, movie theaters, sightseeing, sports venues and more.

Big Apple Greeters

1 Centre Street, Suite 2035
New York, NY 10007
Tel: (212) 669-8159
www.bigapplegreeter.org

Organizes volunteer-led visits to New York City neighborhoods for out-of-town disabled visitors. Volunteer guides are disabled or have done disability-sensibility training. Visits require 4 weeks' notice, the online visit-request-form is the preferred way of signing up.

Mobility International USA / National Clearing House on Disability and Exchange (NCDE)
www.miusa.org

A non-profit organization that focuses on ensuring successful international experiences for people with disabilities. It provides a free information and referral service, including contacts for disability-related organizations worldwide.

Travel in the US

Lonely Planet
www.lonelyplanet.com

Rough Guides
www.roughguides.com

Both websites are "portals" to the guidebooks they sell, but still contain up-to-date and useful information, including comments from other travelers.

National Park Service
www.nps.gov

This website can help you plan a successful visit to a national park; it contains information on opening hours, activities, weather, and more. Most national parks charge entry fees, usually $20 (sometimes less) per vehicle. If you plan on visiting several parks within one year, the "National Parks Pass" ($50, admits purchaser & others in the same vehicle) can be a smart purchase.

Amtrak
Toll Free: (800) USA-RAIL
(Automated service; say "agent" to speak to a person)
www.amtrak.com

The national railroad company. A 15% student discount on most rail fares (2nd class) is available with a Student Advantage Card. There are also rail passes available for non-US passport holders that allow unlimited travel within a specific period of time (5, 15 or 30 days), regional or nationwide. Prices vary form $149 – $550, obtainable at Amtrak ticket offices or online. Some travel agencies also offer 3- and 7-day passes ($99 – $175) for specific regions (www.usbyrail.com). Most trains have a restaurant and a snack-car. Some also have a sightseeing car with videos and informative programs on history and nature.

Greyhound
Toll Free: (800) 229-9424
www.greyhound.com

The largest provider of intercity bus service. 15% student discount is available online and for walk-up tickets (NOT on phone-bookings) with a Student Advantage Card. Greyhound buses are faster and usually cheaper than Amtrak trains, but are less comfortable and not as convenient if you want to enjoy the scenery along the way.

Peter Pan Bus Lines
Toll Free: (800) 237-8747
www.peterpanbus.com

Bonanza Bus
Toll Free: (888) 751-8800
www.bonanzabus.com

Two bus services run by the same company serving the Northeastern region of the U.S. Fares are similar to Greyhound, and a 15% student discount is available with a Student Advantage Card on selected walk-up fares.

Student Advantage Card
www.studentadvantage.com/discountcard

Student discount card necessary to qualify for certain discounts with Amtrak and Greyhound; also good for discounts at a variety of other places (see website). Available for full-time students or young travelers under 26.

TrekAmerica
P.O. Box 189
Rockaway, New Jersey 07866
Tel: (973) 983-1144
Toll Free: (800) 221 0596
Fax: (973) 903-8551
info@trekusasales.com
www.trekamerica.com

TrekAmerica offers experienced small group adventure travel in North America covering the USA, Canada, Alaska & Mexico. TrekAmerica's adventure holidays offer a unique combination of sightseeing and activities that will take you to big cities, National Parks, remote beaches and many other hidden places off the tourist routes. See the best of North America and experience the many adventures this beautiful land has to offer!

American International Tours
Toll Free: (800) 552-3932
www.tourquest.com

American International Tours specializes in student travel to popular destinations in the Northeastern U.S. and Canada, including Boston, Washington DC, Philadelphia, Niagara Falls, Toronto, Montreal, Quebec, Vermont Skiing, Amish Country and more. Tours are designed as weekend getaways for college students and other young adults looking to have fun, meet people, and get away for a while.

Travel CUTS New York
124 MacDougal St.
New York, NY 10012
Tel: (212) 674-CUTS (2887)
Toll Free: (800) 592-CUTS (2887) U.S.
National Reservation Center

Travel CUTS specializes in student budget travel. Book discount airfare, tours, youth hostels, budget hotels, rail passes, and bus passes with Travel CUTS. Student discounts available with the International Student Identity Card (ISIC).

CONSULATES AND MISSIONS

A

Afghanistan
360 Lexington Avenue, 11th Floor
(212) 972-2276
www.embassyofafghanistan.org

Albania
320 East 79th Street
(212) 249-2059
www.albaniaembassy.org/

Algeria
326 East 48th Street
(212) 750-1960
www.algeria-us.org/
www.algeria-un.org

Angola
866 United Nations Plaza
(212) 861-5656
www.angola.org/

Argentina
12 West 56th Street
(212) 603-0400
www.congenargentinany.com/

Armenia
119 East 36th Street
(212) 686-9079
www2.un.int/public/Armenia/
www.armeniaemb.org/

Australia
150 East 42nd Street, 34th Floor
(212) 351-6500
www.australianyc.org/

Austria
31 East 69th Street
(212) 737-6400
www.austria.org
Note: this website is not for the consulate of Austria. However, it does include the Website of Consulate in New York City, and I add this website because the website of consulate is not as informative as the one above.

Azerbaijan
866 United Nations Plaza, Suite 560
(212) 371-2559
www.azembassy.com/
www.un.int/azerbaijan

B

Bahamas, Commonwealth of the
231 East 46th Street
(212) 421-6420
www.un.int/bahamas/

Bahrain
866 Second Avenue United Nations Plaza,
14thFloor
(212) 223-6200
www.bahrainembassy.org/
www2.un.int/public/Bahrain/

Bangladesh, People's Republic of
211 East 43rd Street
(212) 599-6767
www.bangladoot.org/
www.bdcgny.org/

Barbados
800 Second Avenue
(212) 867-8435
www.barbados.org

Belarus
708 Third Avenue, 21st Floor
(212) 682-5392
www.belarusembassy.org/
www.un.int/belarus/

Belgium
1065 Avenue of the Americas, 22nd Floor
(212) 586-5110
www.diplobel.us/
www.diplomatie.be/newyork

Belize
820 Second Avenue, Suite 900
(212) 599-0233
www.embassyofbelize.org/

Bhutan
2 United Nations Plaza, 27th Floor
(212) 826-1919
www.embassy.org/embassies/bt.html

Bolivia
211 East 43rd Street, 8th Floor, Suite 702
(212) 687-0530
www.bolivia-usa.org/
www.bolivia-un.org/

Bosnia and Herzegovina
866 United Nations Plaza, Suite 580
(212) 751-9018
www.un.int/bosnia/
(website under construction)
www.bhembassy.org/Consular_information/
1.html

Botswana
103 E. 37th Street
(212) 889-2277
www.botswanaembassy.org/

Brazil
1185 Sixth Avenue, 21st Floor
(212) 827-0976
www.brazilny.org/

Brunei
866 United Nations Plaza
(212) 697-3465
www.bruneiembassy.org/

Bulgaria, The Republic of
121 East 62nd Street
(212) 935-4646
http://bulgaria-embassy.org/
www.un.int/bulgaria/
www.consulbulgaria-ny.org/

Burkina
115 East 73rd Street
(212) 288-7515
www.burkinaembassy-usa.org/

C

Cambodia, The Kingdom of
866 United Nations Plaza, Room 420
(212) 223-0676
www.embassyofcambodia.org/
www.un.int/cambodia/

Cameroon
22 East 73rd Street
(212) 794-2295
www.ambacam-usa.org

Canada
1251 6th Avenue
(212) 596-1628
www.dfait-maeci.gc.ca/new_york/

Cape Verde
607 Boston Street, 4th Floor
(617) 353-0014
www.un.int/wcm/content/site/capeverde/
pid/3548

Central African Republic
1618 22nd Street, NW
(202) 483-7800

Chad
32002 R Street, NW
(202) 462-4009

Chile
866 United Nations Plaza, Suite 601
(212) 980-3707
www.chile-usa.org
www.un.int/chile

China, Peoples Republic of,
520 Twelfth Avenue
(212) 244-9456
www.nyconsulate.prchina.org/eng/

Colombia
10 East 46th Street
(212) 798-9000
www.colombiaemb.org/
www.consuladodecolombiany.com

Comoros
420 E. 50th Street
(212) 750-1637

Congo
14 East 65th Street
(212) 744-7840

Costa Rica
80 Wall Street
(212) 509-3066
http://costarica-embassy.org/

Croatia
369 Lexington Avenue
(212) 599-3066
www.croatiaemb.org/

Cyprus, Republic of
13 East 40th Street, 5th Floor
(212) 686-6016
www.cyprusembassy.net/

Czech Republic
1109-1111 Madison Avenue
(212) 535-8814
(646) 981-4040
www.mzv.cz/washington

D

Denmark
885 Second Avenue
(212) 223-4545
www.denmark.org/index.htm

Dominican Republic
1501 Broadway, Suite 410
(212) 768-2480
www.domrep.org/

E

Ecuador
800 Second Avenue
(212) 808-0170
www.ecuador.org/

Egypt, Arab Republic of
1110 Second Avenue, Suite 201
(212) 759-7120
www.egyptnyc.net

El Salvador
46 Park Avenue
(212) 889-3608
www.elsalvador.org/

Equatorial Guinea
2020 16th Street NW
(202) 518-5700·

Eritrea
800 Second Avenue, 18th Floor
(212) 687-3390

Estonia
600 Third Avenue, 26th Floor
(212) 883 0636
www.estemb.org/

Ethiopia
866 Second Avenue, 3rd Floor
(212) 421-1830
www.ethiopianembassy.org

F

Fiji
630 Third Avenue, 7th Floor
(212) 687-4130

Finland
866 United Nations Plaza
(212) 750-4400
www.finland.org/

France
934 Fifth Avenue
(212) 606-3600
www.info-france-usa.org/

G

Gabon
18 East 41st Street, 9th Floor
(212) 686-9720
www.un.int/gabon/

Gambia
820 Second Avenue, Suite 900C
(212) 949-6640
http://www2.un.int/public/Gambia/

Georgia
One United Nations Plaza, 26th Floor
(212) 759-1949
www.georgiaemb.org/

Germany, Federal Republic of
871 United Nations Plaza
(212) 610-9700
www.germany-info.org

Ghana
19 East 47th Street
(212) 832-1300
www.ghana-embassy.org/

Greece
69 East 79th Street
(212) 988-5500
www.greekembassy.org

Grenada
800 Second Avenue, Suite 400k
(212) 599-0301
http://grenadaconsulate.org

Guatemala
57 Park Avenue, Suite 401
(212) 686-3837
http://guatemala.un.int/english/english.html

Guyana, Republic of
370 Seventh Avenue
(212) 947-5115
www.guyana.org/

Guinea
140 E 39th Street
(212) 687-8115
www.un.int/guinea/Guinea_pgs/mst_fm6.htm

Guinea-Bissau
15929 Yukon Lane, Rockville
(301) 947-3958

H

Haiti
271 Madison Avenue
(212) 697-9767
www.haiti.org/hatianconsulate-nyc.org

Honduras
35 West 35 Street, 6th Floor
(212) 714-9450
www.hondurasemb.org/

Hong Kong
520 Twelfth Avenue
(212) 244-9456
(212) 244-9392
www.china-embassy.org/eng/default.htm

Hungary
223 East 52nd Street
(212) 752-0661
www.humisny.org/

I

Iceland
800 Third Avenue, 36th Floor
(212) 593-2700
www.iceland.org/us/nyc.

India
3 East 64th Street
(212) 774-0662
www.indiacgny.org/
www.indianembassy.org/

Indonesia
5 East 68th Street
(212) 879-0600
http://indonesianewyork.org

Iran
622 Third Avenue
(212) 687-2020
www.un.int/iran/
www.daftar.org

Iraq
14 East 79th Street
(212) 737-4433
http://iraqunmission.org

Ireland
345 Park Avenue
(212) 319-2555
www.irelandemb.org/
http://consulateofirelandnewyork.org

Israel
800 Second Avenue
(212) 499-5000
www.israelfm.org/

Italy
690 Park Avenue
(212) 439-8600
www.consnewyork.esteri.it

Ivory Coast
46 East 74th Street
(212) 717-5555

J

Jamaica
767 Third Avenue
(212) 935-9000
http://congenjamaica-ny.org

Japan
299 Park Avenue
(212) 371-8222
www.ny.us.emb-japan.go.jp/

Jordan
866 United Nations Plaza
(212) 832-9553
www.un.int/jordan

K

Kazakhstan
305 East 47th Street, 3rd Floor
(212) 888 3024
www.kazconsulny.org

Kenya
866 United Nations Plaza, Room 4014
(212) 421-4740
www.kenyaembassy.com/nyconsulate.html

Korea, Republic of
460 Park Avenue
(212) 692-9120
www.koreanconsulate.org

Kuwait
321 East 44th Street
(212) 973-4318
http://kuwaitmission.com

Kyrgyzstan
866 United Nations Plaza Suite 477
(212) 486-4214
www.kgembassy.org/
http://kyrgyzstan.org/

Laos
317 East 51st Street
(212) 832-2734
www.laoembassy.com/laomission

Latvia
333 East 50 th. StreetU
(212) 838-8877
http://un.int/latvia

Lebanon
9 East 76th Street
(212) 744-7905
www.lebanonembassyus.org/
http://lebconsny.org

Lesotho
204 East 39th Street
(212) 661-1690
www.un.int/lesotho/

Liberia
820 Second Avenue
(212) 687-1025

Libya
309 East 48th Street
(212) 752-5775
www.libya-watanona.com/libya1/embassy.
htm

Lithuania
420 Fifth Avenue
(212) 354-7840
www.ltembassyus.org/
www.un.int//lithuania/lithuania.html

Luxembourg
17 Beekman Place
(212) 888-6664
www.luxembourgnyc.org/

M

Macedonia
866 United Nations Plaza
(212) 308-8504
http://macedonia-un.org

Madagascar
801 Second Avenue
(212) 986-9491
www.embassy.org/madagascar/

Malaysia
313 East 43rd Street
(212) 490-2722
www.un.int/malaysia/

Maldives
800 Second Avenue, Suite 400E
(212) 599-6195
http://maldivesmission-ny.com/eng

Malta
249 East 35th Street
(212) 725-2345
www.foreign.gov.mt

Mali
111 East 69th Street
(212) 737-4150
www2.un.int/public/Mali/

Marshall Island
800 2nd Ave. 18th Floor
(212) 983-3040
www.rmiembassyus.org/
www2.un.int/public/Marshall_Islands/

Mauritania
116 East 38th Street
(212) 252-0113
www.maurinet.com/embasydc.html
www2.un.int/public/mauritania

Mauritius
211 East 43rd Street
(212) 949-0190
www.maurinet.com/embasydc.html
www.un.int/mauritius/

Mexico
27 East, 39th Street
(212) 217-6400
http://portal.sre.gob.mx/usa

Micronesia
820 Second Avenue, Suite 17A
(212) 697-8370
http://fsmgov.org
www.fsmembassydc.org/mission.htm

Moldova
35 East 29th Street
(212) 447-1867
www.un.int/moldova/

Monaco
565 Fifth Avenue
(212) 286-0500
www.monaco-consulate.com
www.monaco-un.org/

Mongolia
6 East 77th Street
(212) 861-9460
www.un.int/mongolia

Morocco, Kingdom of
767 Third Avenue, Floor 30
(212) 421-1580
www.maroc.net

Mozambique
420 East 50th Street
(212) 644-6800
www.un.int/mozambique

Myanmar, The Union of
10 East 77th Street
(212) 535-1310
www.mewashingtondc.com/

N

Namibia
135 East 36th street
(212) 685-2003
www.embassy.org/embassies/na.html
www.namibianembassyusa.org/

Nepal
820 Second Avenue
(212) 370-4188
www.nepalembassyusa.org/

Netherlands
235 East 45th Street, 9th Floor
(212) 697-5547
www.cgny.org/homepage.asp

New Zealand
1 UN Plaza, 25th Floor
(212) 826-1960
www.nzembassy.com/home.cfm?c=31

Nicaragua
820 Second Avenue
(212) 490-7997
www.un.int/nicaragua/

Niger
417 East 50th Street
(212) 421-3260
www.nigerembassyusa.org/
www.un.int/niger/

Nigeria
828 Second Avenue
(212) 808-0301
www.nigeriaembassyusa.org
www.un.int/nigeria

Norway
825 Third Avenue
(212) 421-0380
www.norway.org

O

Oman
866 United Nations Plaza
(212) 355-3505
www.un.int/wcm/content/site/oman

P

Pakistan
8 East 65th Street
(212) 879-8600
http://pakistanconsulateny.org

Panama
866 UN Plaza
(212) 421-5420
http://nyconsul.com/

Papua New Guinea,
201 East 42nd Street, Suite 405
(212) 557-5001
www.pngembassy.org/

Paraguay
211 East 43rd Street
(212) 687-3490
www.embaparusa.gov.py/
www.un.int/paraguay

Peru
829 Second Avenue
(212) 687-3336
www.peruvianembassy.us/
www.un.int/wcm/content/site/peru

Philippines, Republic of
556 Fifth Avenue
(212) 764-1300
www.philippineembassy-usa.org/
www.un.int/philippines/

Poland, Republic of
9 East 66th Street
(212) 744-2506
www.polandembassy.org/
www.polishconsulateny.org

Portugal
866 Second Avenue
(212) 759-9444
www.un.int/portugal/

Q

Qatar
809 United Nations Plaza, 4th Floor
(212) 486-9335
www.qatarembassy.net/

R

Romania
537 Third Avenue
(212) 682-3273
www.romconsny.org/
http://mpnewyork.mae.ro/

Russian Federation
136 East 67th Street
(212) 861-4900
www.ruscon.com/

Rwanda
124 East 39th Street
(212) 696-0644
www2.un.int/public/Rwanda

S

Saint Kitts & Nevis
414 East 75th Street, 5th Floor
(212) 535-1234
www.stkittsnevis.org/

Saint Lucia
820 Second Avenue
(212) 697-9360
www.un.int/stlucia/

Saint Vincent & The Grenadines
801 Second Avenue
(212) 687-4490
www.un.int/wcm/content/site/stvincent

San Marino
186 Lehrer, Elmont, NY 11003
(212) 751-1234

Sao Tome & Principe
400 Park Avenue
(212) 317-0533

Saudi Arabia
405 Lexington Avenue
(212) 697-4830
www.saudiembassy.net/
www.saudi-un-ny.net

Senegal
238 East 68th Street
(212) 517-9030
www.un.int/senegal/

Serbia
854 Fifth Avenue
(212) 879-8700
www.un.int/serbia

Seychelles
820 Second Avenue
(212) 972-1785
www.un.int/wcm/content/site/seychelles

Sierra Leone
245 East 49th Street
(212) 688-1656
www.un.int/sierraleone/

Singapore
231 East 51st Street
(212) 826-0840
www.mfa.gov.sg/washington/
http://mfa.sg/newyork/

Slovakia
801 Second Avenue
(212) 286-8880
www.slovakembassy-us.org/

Slovenia
600 Third Avenue
(212) 370-3007
http://newyork.predstavnistvo.si/en

South Africa
333 East 38th Street
(212) 213-5583
www.southafrica-newyork.net/

Spain
150 East 58th Street
(212) 355-4080
www.spainconsul-ny.org/
www.maec.es/subwebs/consulados/
nuevayork/es/home/Paginas/Home.aspx

Sri Lanka
630 Third Avenue
(212) 986-7040
www.slembassyusa.org/

Sudan, the Republic of
733 Third Avenue
(212) 573-6033
www.sudanembassy.org/

Surinam
866 United Nations Plaza
(212) 826-0660
www.surinameembassy.org/
www.un.int/wcm/content/site/suriname

Swaziland
408 East 50th Street
(212) 371-8910
www.un.int/wcm/content/site/swaziland

Sweden
885 Second Avenue
(212) 583-2500
www.swedenabroad.com

Switzerland
633 Third Avenue
(212) 285-1540
www.swissemb.org
www.eda.admin.ch/missny

Syria
820 Second Avenue
(212) 661-1313
www.syrianembassy.us/
www.un.int/syria/

T ─────────────────────

Taiwan
1 East, 42nd Street, 11th. Floor
(212) 557-5122
http://taiwanembassy.org/US/NYC/
mp.asp?mp=62

Tanzania
201 East 42nd Street
(212) 972-9160
www.tanzaniaembassy-us.org/
www.tanzania-un.org

Thailand
351 East 52nd Street
(212) 754-2230
www.thaiembdc.org
http://thaiconsulnewyork.com

Togo Republic
112 East 40th Street
(212) 490-3455

Trinidad & Tobago
820 Second Avenue
(212) 697-7620
http://ttembassy.cjb.net/

Tunisia
1 Battery Park Pz.
(212) 742-6585
www.tunisiaonline.com/tunisia-un/index.html

Turkey
821 United Nations Plaza
(212) 949-0150
www.turkishembassy.org/start.html
www.un.int/turkey

Turkmenistan
866 United Nations Plaza, Suite 424
(212) 486-8908
www.turkmenistanembassy.org/
www2.un.int/public/Turkmenistan/

Ukraine
240 East 49th Street
(212) 371-5690
www.ukrconsul.org/

United Arab Emirates
305 East 47th Street, 7th Floor
(212) 371-0480
www.un.int/uae/

United Kingdom
885 Second Avenue
(212) 745-9200
www.britainusa.com/ny/

Uruguay
866 UN Plaza
(212) 752-8240
www.uruwashi.org/
www.un.int/uruguay

Uzbekistan, Republic of
866 United Nations Plaza
(212) 486-4242
www.uzbekistan.org/

V

Venezuela
335 East 46th Street
(212) 557-2055
www.newyork.embavenez-us.org/

Vietnam
866 United Nations Plaza, Suite 435
(212) 644-0594
www.vietnamembassy-usa.org/
www.vietnam-un.org/en/index.php

Yemen
413 East 51st Street
(213) 355-1730
www.yemenembassy.org/
www.un.int/wcm/content/site/yemen

Yugoslavia
855 Fifth Avenue (See Serbia and Montenegro)
(212) 879-8700

Z

Zambia
237 East 52nd Street
(212) 888-5770
www.un.int/zambia/

Zimbabwe
128 East 56th Street
(212) 980-9511
www2.un.int/public/Zimbabwe/

NAVIGATING NYC

Manhattan Street Design

New York City may strike the newcomer as a difficult place to navigate, but if you have a basic idea of the geography of the city and learn the different forms of transportation, then getting around will become easy.

Manhattan streets are laid out in a grid pattern, with avenues running north and south (uptown and downtown) and streets east and west (crosstown). Fifth Avenue divides Manhattan into the east and west sides. South of 4th Street in the Village, the streets follow an irregular pattern and have names instead of numbers.

Get yourself a good street map (available in bookstores); this will be especially useful for finding locations in NYC's other boroughs—Brooklyn, Queens, The Bronx, and Staten Island. Or go on line to a service like Mapquest **www.mapquest.com**.

Key to Manhattan Street Addresses

To determine which avenue is nearest to a street address, use the following chart.

Example: 356 West 34th Street is located between 8th and 9th Avenues.

East Side
- 1 at 5th Avenue
- 101 at Park or 4th Avenue
- 201 at 3rd Avenue
- 301 at 2nd Avenue
- 401 at 1st Avenue
- 501 at York Avenue or Avenue A
- 601 at Avenue B

West Side
- 1 at 5th Avenue
- 101 at 6th Avenue (6th Avenue is also called Avenue of the Americas south of Central Park)
- 201 at 7th Avenue
- 301 at 8th Avenue
- 4 1 at 9th Avenue (9th Avenue is called Columbus Avenue north of 59th Street)

To determine the approximate cross street for addresses located on the avenues, try the following formula:
- Cancel the last figure of the house number
- Divide the remainder by two
- Then add or subtract the key number below. The result is approximately the nearest cross street.

Example: 350 Park Avenue is located near what street?
- Drop the last figure (0)
- Divide by 2 (=17)
- Then add the key number (for Park Avenue this is 34). This address is located near 51st Street (17 + 34 = 51).

Key Numbers for Streets and Avenues

Avenue A – D	Add 3
1st and 2nd Avenue	Add 3
3rd Avenue	Add 10
4th Avenue	Add 8
Park Avenue South	Add 8
5th Avenue	
• Up to 200	Add 13
• Up to 400	Add 16
• Up to 600	Add 18
• Up to 775	Add 20
• From 775 to 1286	Cancel last figure, subtract 18
• Up to 1500	Add 45
• Above 2000	Add 24
6th Avenue (Avenue of the Americas)	Subtract 12
7th Avenue	
• 1 to 1800	Add 12
• Above 1800	Add 20
8th Avenue	Add 9
9th Avenue	Add 13
10th Avenue	Add 14
11th Avenue	Add 15
Amsterdam Avenue	Add 59
Audubon Avenue	Add 165
Broadway	
• Up to 754	Below 8th Street
• 756 to 846	Subtract 29
• 847 to 953	Subtract 25
• Above 953	Subtract 31
Columbus Ave	Add 59 or 60
Convent Ave	Add 127
Fort Washington Avenue	Add 158
Lenox Avenue	Add 10
Lexington Avenue	Add 22
Madison Avenue	Add 27
Manhattan Avenue	Add 100
Park Avenue	Add 34
Park Avenue South	Add 8
St. Nicholas Avenue	Add 110
West End Avenue	Add 59
Central Park West	Divide by 10 and add 60
Riverside Drive	Divide by 10 and add 72

3 3-room apartment: kitchen, living room, and bedroom (plus bath)

4 4-room apartment: kitchen, living room and 2 bedrooms (plus bath)

A/C Air conditioned

AG; AGENCY Agent; an individual or company appointed by the apartment owner to manage the building, collect rents, etc.

ALCV Alcove; section of a living room that can be sectioned off to create a small dining area or bedroom

APT Apartment

AVAIL Available

BARS Security against break-ins when placed over windows

BDRM; BRM; BR Bedroom

BKR; BROKER An agent appointed by the landlord to show apartments to prospective tenants and to negotiate leases. A broker will charge the new tenant a fee for his or her services.

BLDG Building

BRNSTN Brownstone; a 3–5 floor building, usually without an elevator, so named because of the traditional brown stone or brick facade

CEIL Ceiling

CLSTS Closets

COL U Columbia University area

COED Both males and females

CO-OP / CONDO Two different types of apartment buildings where individual apartments are owned, rather than rented, by the building's residents

CONV TRANS Convenient to transportation

CNV Convertible; usually refers to a space, such as a dining room or alcove, that can be converted into a bedroom

CPN Central Park North

CPW Central Park West

DA Dining area

DEC FP Decorative (i.e., nonworking) fireplace

DR Dining room

DRMN Doorman; a person employed by the landlord and who is stationed at the main entrance to admit visitors, provide security, and assist tenants by accepting deliveries and hailing taxis

DUMBO Down Under the Manhattan Bridge Overpass (area of Brooklyn)

D / W Dishwasher

EIK Eat-in kitchen; a kitchen large enough to hold a table and chairs

EFFICIENCY; EFF A studio apartment (see "STUDIO" below)

ELEC Electric or electricity

ELEV Elevator

EV East Village

EXPOSED; EXPSD BRICK Wall from which plaster has been removed to expose the underlying brick construction

FAB Fabulous

FIX FEE Fixture fee; the tenant must pay a set fee for the appliances provided in the dwelling (e.g., tub, sink, toilet, etc.). This fee is usually charged on loft rentals only.

FL BTH Full Bath (toilet, sink, tub or shower) as opposed to a half bath (toilet and sink only)

FLEX Flexible (same as "CONVERTIBLE," see above)

FLTRN Flat Iron (area around 5th Ave. and 23rd St)

FLR; FL Floor

FLR-THRU Floor-through; an apartment that occupies an entire floor of a building

FPLC; FPL Fireplace

FR From

FULL KIT Full kitchen; a kitchen with a full-sized stove, sink, and refrigerator

FURN Furnished, meaning that the apartment is already supplied with furniture and kitchenware

GAR Garage

GAY Homosexual

G / E Gas and electricity

GP / GRAM Gramercy Park (area around Lexington Ave. and lower 20's)

GRT Great

HARDWD; HW Hardwood Floors

HI CEILS High ceilings; an apartment in which the ceilings are at least 10 feet high.

IMM OCC Immediate occupancy; apartment is available immediately

INCL Includes or including

INTERCOM A two-way communication system with microphone and speaker or telephone, which enables tenants to admit visitors while keeping the main door locked

JR Junior; refers to an apartment in which the living room can be subdivided to create a small bedroom

KIT / KITCH Kitchen

LANDLORD / LADY The person who owns the apartment building and to whom the rent is paid

LEASE A legal document signed by both the landlord and the tenant, specifying the rent and duration that the premises will be rented; also a verb, meaning to rent

LEX Lexington Avenue

LOC Location

LRG; LG Large

LNDRY Laundry

LOFT An industrial space that has been converted into a living space; usually larger than a regular apartment

LUX; LUXURY Refers to a full-service apartment with a 24-hour doorman, laundry room, elevator, and high rent

LVRM; LRM; LR Living room

MO Monthly

MOD APPL Modern appliances

NO FEE No charge to prospective tenant by a real estate agent or broker

NOHO North of Houston Street

NOLITA North of Little Italy

NON-SMOKER A person who does not smoke cigarettes

NR Near

NU New

NWLY REN Newly renovated

ORIG Original

OWNER / MGMT Owner / Management; the owner manages the building rather than designating an agent as intermediary; Often no fee

OWNER OCC Owner occupied; the owner lives in the building, which usually means the building is safe and well maintained

PATIO A paved courtyard

PENTHOUSE; PH An apartment on the top floor of a building, usually with a terrace

PK VU Park view

PREM Premises

PREWAR; P-WAR An apartment building constructed before World War II; usually means large rooms with high ceilings

PVT BATH Private bathroom

PVT RM Private room

PULLMAN KIT Pullman kitchen; small kitchen area that extends along one wall and can usually be closed off by a sliding or folding door

REFS REQ'D References required

REN; RENO; RENV Renovated

RIV VU River view

RM Room

ROOMMATE A person or persons with whom one shares a living space

RR FLAT Railroad flat; an apartment that requires passing through each room to get to the next

SEC Security deposit

SEP KIT Separate kitchen

SF   Square feet

SHARE   An arrangement whereby one rents an apartment with someone who already lives in the apartment

SL ALCOVE   Sleeping alcove; area (usually in a studio) large enough for a bed, not a separate room but set off from the main living space

SLEEP LOFT   A platform at least 6 feet above the floor, containing a bed; often found in studios where it is used to maximize floor space

SLPING   Sleeping

SOBRO   South Bronx

SO EX   Southern exposure; the apartment faces south, receiving good sunlight

SOHO   South of Houston Street

SPAC   Spacious

STRAIGHT   Heterosexual

STUDIO; STUD   A one-room apartment (bedroom and living room combined) with a separate bathroom; kitchen may be part of the living space or a separate room

STY   Story or floor

SUBLET   A procedure by which the legal tenant of an apartment rents this space to someone else

SUBW; SBW   Subway

SUPER   Superintendent; person employed by the landlord to keep the building in good condition, usually residing in the building or at a nearby address

T1   Denotes building cabled for a high speed Internet connection in every apartment

TENANT   The person who rents an apartment from the landlord

TENEMENT   An unrenovated building with many apartments, most of which open out onto an air shaft

TERR   Terrace, patio, or balcony

TH   Townhouse (see "TWNHSE" below)

TIK   Tub in kitchen; denotes an apartment in which the bathtub is located in the kitchen (toilet and sink separate); usually found only in older tenements (see "TENEMENT" above)

TRIBECA   Triangle Below Canal Street; (area south of SoHo on the west side

24-HR DRMN   An apartment security service; the doorman is on duty 24 hours a day

TWNHSE   A small (usually 3 to 5 floors) apartment building, usually without an elevator

UTIL   Utilities (gas and electricity)

UTIL INCL   Utilities are included in the monthly rent

UES   Upper East Side

UWS   Upper West Side

VIC   In the vicinity of; near a designated landmark or location

VU   View; the apartment looks out on a pleasant view

W/   With

WALK-UP   A building of 2 to 6 floors without an elevator

WBF; WBFP   Wood-burning (i.e., working) fireplace

WDFLRS   Wood Floors

WEA   West End Avenue

WIND KITA   Kitchen with a window

WLK-IN CLOSET   A closet that is large enough to walk into

W/UTIL   With utilities; rent includes the cost of gas and electricity

WV; W.Vill   West Village

XLNT   Excellent

XPOS BRK   Exposed brick

XTRA   Extra

Short-Term Accommodations (W&M)

Name	Daily Rates	Notes
1291 ACCOMMODATION (212) 397-9686 337 West 55th Street New York, NY 10019 Fax: (212) 397-1494 www.1291.com 1291@1291.com	Budget Stay $65 Basic Stay $175 New-Yorker Stay $190	Private suites available upon request. Safety deposit lockers ($2 per stay) are provided, linens, blankets, and towels included. Common dining area with refrigerator, microwave & TV. Washing machine & dryer. Office featuring copiers, printers, fax & Internet service. Passport & ID required for check in. Maximum stay: 28 days.
AMSTERDAM INN (212) 579-7500 340 Amsterdam Avenue New York, NY 10024 Fax: (212) 579-6127 www.amsterdaminn.com amsterdaminn@nyinns.com	**Full or Twin w / shared bath** $109 **Queen w / shared bath** Starting at $129 **Rooms w / private bath** $149 – $205	Advanced reservations required. Color/cable TV, telephones, air conditioning, 24-hour concierge, multilingual staff, fax & copy service at front desk. Complementary continental breakfast, daily maid service, kitchenettes, pool and gym access, high speed DSL and dial up internet available.
AMERICAN DREAM HOSTEL (212) 260-9779 168 East 24th Street New York City, NY 10010 Fax: (212) 260-9944 www.americandreamhostel.com americandream24@aol.com	Dormitory (up to 4 people) $47.50 / person **Private Single** $75 / person Shared bathroom for all rooms	Family owned and run business. The owner speaks English, Spanish, Portuguese and Italian. Prices include breakfast, linen and towels. The hostel provides air conditioning and internet access.
BIG APPLE HOSTEL (212) 302-2603 119 West 45th Street New York, NY 10036 Fax: (212) 302-2605 www.bigapplehostel.com mail@bigapplehostel.com	Dormitory $39 – $60 **Private room** $125 – $175 All taxes included	24 hour reception, free linen, air conditioning, lockers for valuables, laundry room, international call and fax service, common room, internet access, fully equipped kitchen, backyard with BBQ. Cash and credit only, no travelers checks. Maximum stay: 21 days.

Short-Term Accommodations (W&M)

Name	Daily Rates	Notes
BOWERY'S WHITEHOUSE HOTEL OF NY (212) 477-5623 340 Bowery Street New York, NY 10012 www.whitehousehotelofny.com reservations@ whitehousehotelofny.com	Single $27.94 – $29.57 Double $53.90 – $56.50 Triple $70.84 – $81.49 Shared bathroom for all rooms	Shared bathrooms. All rooms are air conditioned. Linens and towels included. Great lounge with microwave & refrigerator. International pay phone for low cost U.S. and Worldwide Calls. 42 inch cable TV color projection with DVD and free movies. Internet access, wireless internet available for laptops. Cable TV in private rooms available. Laundry facilities. Private safety boxes available. Fresh coffee, tea.
BROADWAY HOTEL & HOSTEL (212) 865-7710 230 West 101 Street New York, NY 10025 Fax: (212) 865-2993 www.broadwayhotelnyc.com reservations@ broadwayhotelnyc.com	**Private rooms** $150 – $300 per night not including tax **Dormitory / shared rooms** $18 – $50 per night not including tax	Rooms contain sinks. Standard rooms have shared baths. Private facilities are available at an additional charge. High-speed internet access in the lobby. Lift/ elevator available for physically challenged. Complimentary linens, towels, and blankets, for your convenience. Daily housekeeping service for all our guests. Maximum stay: 14 days.
CARLTON ARMS HOTEL (212) 679-0680 160 East 25th Street New York, NY 10010 www.carltonarms.com/ artbreakhotel@aol.com	**Daily / Weekly w / private bathroom** Single $110 / $693 Double $130 / $820 Triple $155 / $977 Quad $180 / $1,134 **w / shared bath** Single $80 / $504 Double $110 / $693 Triple $140 / $882	Rates listed apply to students & foreign travelers. Each room with shared bathroom has a sink. There is a separate toilet and a shower room in every hall for guests to use privately. We don't have room service but provide fresh towels or linen at guests request. No TV or phone in the rooms—available in common room. Internet service available. Cash, travelers checks and credit card. Pay for seven or more nights upon arrival and receive a 10% discount.

Short-Term Accommodations (W&M)

Name	Daily Rates	Notes
CENTRAL PARK HOSTEL (212) 678-0491 19 West 103rd Street New York, NY 10025 Fax: (212) 678-0453 www.centralparkhostel.com info@centralparkhostel.com	**Dormitory rooms** **w /shared bathroom** $34 – $40 **Private rooms** **w/shared bathroom** $89 – $119 per night **Studio Apartments** $109 – $179	All rooms are air conditioned. We provide all linens, we do not provide towels for dormitory rooms and all rooms have lockers. Our maximum stay is 13 day's. Cash or travelers checks only. No credit cards. Foreign passports required upon check-in. Tours and airport transfers can be booked at front desk. 24-hour security, linens included, air-conditioning, lockers, recreation room (pool table), & TV lounge.
CHELSEA INTERNATIONAL HOSTEL (212) 647-0010 251 West 20th Street New York, NY 10011 Fax: (212) 727-7289 www.chelseahostel.com reservations@chelseahostel.com	Dormitory w / shared bathroom $32 w / private bathroom $36 **Private room** (2 people max) w / shared bathroom $80	Discount rates of $23 for dorms and $58 for privates including tax for groups of 20 people or more. All groups must be paid prior to arrival. $10 CASH key deposit required at check in which will be refunded upon check out. Credit Card, Travelers Checks or Cash payments. All payments are due upon check in. Reservation with only credit card. Hostel provides linens, but no towels. Lockers are available, bring own lock. Common kitchen area with coffee and tea available. Recreation room with TV, courtyard, internet access, laundry facility.
CHELSEA SAVOY HOTEL (212) 929-9353 204 West 23rd Street New York, NY 10011 Fax: (212) 741-6309 www.chelseasavoy.com chelseasavoy@juno.com	Single (1 double bed) $99 – $125 Double (1 queen bed) $145 – $375 Quad (2 double beds) $155 – $395 King room $185 – $425	Each room equipped with a private bath, cable television, and goose down pillows included. Continental breakfast. Credit card number and expiration date are needed in order to make a reservation. No penalty if cancellation made 24 hours in advance. Group rates available.

Short-Term Accommodations (W&M)

Name	Daily Rates	Notes
COLONIAL HOUSE INN (212) 243-9669 (800) 689-3779 318 West 22nd Street New York, NY 10011 Fax: (212) 633-1612 www.colonialhouseinn.com houseinn@aol.com	Economy (full bed w / shared bath) $130 Standard (queen bed w / shared bath) $150 Deluxe (queen bed w / private bath) $180	Welcomes both gay and straight visitors. Rates include a continental breakfast. Features rooftop patio and an internet access. Rooms equipped with sink, satellite TV. Some rooms have fridges and / or fireplaces. Special weekly and winter rates available. Advance reservations are suggested.
FLUSHING YMCA (718) 961-6880 x133 138-46 Northern Boulevard Flushing, NY 11354 Fax: (718) 445-8392 www.ymcanyc.org flushingguestrooms@ymcanyc.org	**Daily / Weekly** Single $61 / $366 Double $72 / $432 Triple $80 / $550 Shared bathroom for all rooms	Clean, comfortable, safe and very affordable guest rooms with daily housekeeping services, air conditioning and cable TV. Handicap accessible. Easily accessible by public transportation. Special student price of $700 for a month (w / student ID). YMCA facilities also available (pool, sauna, gym)
GERSHWIN HOTEL (212) 545-8000 7 East 27th Street New York, NY 10016 Fax: (212) 684-5546 www.gershwinhotel.com askus@gershwinhotel.com	**Dormitory rooms w / shared bathrooms** 10 beds $34 6 beds $44 4 beds $48 **Private** $109 – $145 **Suites** Family $249 – $385 One-Bedroom Suites $219 – $335	Private rooms have color TV, air-conditioning, hair dryer, iron & ironing board and safe deposit boxes. Baby-sitting, wireless internet access, laundry and discounted parking available for an additional fee.
GISELE'S GUEST HOUSE (212) 666-0559 134 West 119th Street New York, NY 10026 Fax: (212) 663-5000 www.nygiselebnb.com info@nygiseleguesthouse.com	Double $105 – $125 Shared bathroom for all rooms	Manager Gisele Allard can help students find long-term accomidations upon request. Maximum stay: 7 days.
GREENPOINT YMCA (718) 389-3700 99 Meserole Avenue Brooklyn, NY 11222 Fax: (718) 389-2146 www.ymcanyc.org/index. php?id=1167 grpbnb@ymcanyc.org	**Economy room** Single $48 **Deluxe rooms** Single $68 Double $79 Triple $93 Quad $100	TV, radio alarm clock and mailbox access. Indoor swimming pool with male and female suanas, daily houskeeping service, and state-of-the-art fitness center.

Short-Term Accommodations (W&M)

Name	Daily Rates	Notes
HARLEM YMCA (212) 281-4100 x210 180 West 135th Street New York, NY 10030 Fax: (212) 491-3178 www.ymcanyc.org harlemguestrooms@ymcanyc.org	Single $75 Double $100 Student $250 / week (proof needed) Shared bathroom for all rooms	Rooms include TV and air conditioning. Heated swimming pool, weight room, cardiovascular and strength training center. 24-hour security and housekeeping services.
HOSTELLING INTERNATIONAL (212) 932-2300 891 Amsterdam Avenue New York, NY 10025 Fax: (212) 932-2574 www.hinewyork.org	**Dormitory rooms** 4 beds $36 6 – 8 beds $35 10 – 12 beds $32 **Private room** $135 **Family room** $120	Fully equipped kitchen, laundry room and game room. Linens, pillows and blankets included. Common room, meals, garden, luggage storage, internet access, lockers and TV available. Guests must present a driver's liscence or passport at check-in. Mixed and single-sex dorms are available. Handicapped accessible and credit cards accepted.
INTERNATIONAL HOUSE (212) 316-8400 500 Riverside Drive New York, NY 10027 Fax: (212) 316-1827 www.ihouse-nyc.org admissions@ihouse-nyc.org	**Rooms** Single $130 Doubles $150 Triples $165 **Suites** Single $140 Double $160 Triple $175 Quad $190	Open to full-time graduate students only during academic year; undergraduates welcome in summer. Application necessary for stays of 30 days or more. Handicapped accessible.
INTERNATIONAL STUDENT CENTER (212) 787-7706 38 West 88th Street New York, NY 10024 www.nystudentcenter.org info@nystudentcenter.org	Dorms $30 / night November – April Dorms $20 / night	Single sex and co-ed rooms. Internet access, linens, storage area and lockers are available. Full kitchen and common lounge with TV and telephone.
JAZZ ON THE PARK (212) 932-1600 36 West 106th Street New York, NY 10025 Fax: (212) 932-1700 www.jazzhostels.com navy@jazzhostels.com	**Rooms** Double $45 Quad $32 **Dorms** 6 – 8 beds $29 10 – 14 beds $25	Rooms include air conditioning, linens, towels, blankets and light breakfast. Features Jazz Café and coffee bar, roof terrace and garden and internet access. Maximum stay: 14 days.

Short-Term Accommodations (W&M)

Name	Daily Rates	Notes
LANDMARK GUEST ROOMS— UNION THEOLOGICAL SEMINARY (212) 280-1313 3041 Broadway New York, NY 10027 Fax: (212) 280-1488 www.utsnyc.edu landmark@uts.columbia.edu	Single $135 Double $165	Private bath; Cable television; Wireless Internet access; Iron and hair dryer; Miniature refrigerator; Daily housekeeping services; 24-hour access front-desk security; Free local telephone service and all incoming calls. (Guests are requested to use a cell phone or phone card for long-distance calls.)
LARCHMONT HOTEL (212) 989-9333 27 West 11th Street New York, NY 10011 Fax: (212) 989-9496 www.larchmonthotel.com	**Rooms (w / shared bathroom)** Single $90 – $109 Double $119 – $129 Queen $149 **Family room (w / private bathroom)** $219 weekend rates vary	Rooms include TV, telephone, robes and sink. Continental breakfast and shared kitchenettes are available. Rates higher on weekends.
MORNINGSIDE INN (212) 316-0055 235 West 107th Street New York City, NY 10025 Fax: (212)-864-9155 www.morningsideinn-ny.com/ info@morningsideinn-ny.com	Budget $95 Single $85 Double $100 Triple $105 Inquire about private bathrooms	Deluxe rooms and apartment suites are available. Budget rooms include a refrigerator, ceiling fan, telephone, cable TV and are PC accessible. Bathroom and kitchen facilities are shared. Coin operated washer & dryer. Maximum stay: three months.
MURRAY HILL INN (212) 683-6900 143 East 30th Street New York, NY 10016 Fax: (212) 545-0103 www.murrayhillinn.com murrayhillinns@nyinns.com	Single $149 Double $159 – $229 Shared or private bathroom	Reservations necessary. Cash or travelers checks only. Weekly singles subject to availability. Maximum stay: 14 days.
NORTH BROOKLYN YMCA (718) 277-1600 570 Jamaica Avenue Brooklyn, NY 11208 Fax: (718) 277-2081 http://www.ymcanyc.org/index. php?id=1139 nshiwram@ymcanyc.org	Daily $40 Weekly $280 Shared bathroom for all rooms	Private rooms with shared baths. Reservations must be made at least 3 days in advance. Maximum stay: 28 days.

Sara's Homestay

Your Quality Short Term Accommodation Specialist

Providing:
Homestays, Shared Apartments, Private Furnished Apartments,
and Residence Hall rooms

To:
Students, Interns, Visitors, Schools and Agents

In:
New York City and other locations around the world

<u>**Contact us:**</u>
Sara's New York Homestay, LLC
1 West 34th Street, Suite 702
New York, NY 10001
Tel: (212) 564-5979
Fax: (212) 564-0475
info@sarahomestay.com
www.sarahomestay.com

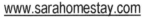

Short-Term Accommodations (W&M)

Name	Daily Rates	Notes
SARA'S NY HOMESTAY (212) 564-5979 1 West 34th Street New York, NY 10001 Fax: (212) 564-0475 www.sarahomestay.com sara@sarahomestay.com	**Standard Single** **(w / breakfast)** 1 week $805 2 weeks $950 3 weeks $1,500 4 weeks $1,500 Inquire about executive single rates.	Private rooms with self served breakfast, sharing with a family or a roommate. Shared and private bathrooms available. Furnished apartments for individuals also available. Double rooms subject to availability. $100 registration fee. Airport pick-up and drop-off available. Minimum stay: 7 nights Maximum stay: up to four years.
SEAFARER INTERNATIONAL HOUSE (212) 677-4800 123 East 15th Street New York, NY 10003 www.sihnyc.org res@sihnyc.org	**Rooms** **w / shared bathroom** Single $82 Double $102 **w / private bathroom** Single $111 Double $131	Advance reservations required. Visa / MasterCard to guarantee reservation. Students must bring letter from their school verifying current registration and a valid student ID card for student discount rate. Maximum stay: 21 days. Our guesthouse features air conditioned & smoke free accommodations, color TV and full cable service, private telephones with voice mail, internet access, coffee bar, library, linen service.
THREE EAST THIRD CORPORATION (212) 533-7749 3 East 3rd Street New York, NY 10003 Fax: (212) 673-5387 www.3E3dorm.com yloria@3e3dorm.com	**Weekly** Single $240 Shared bathroom for all rooms	Reservations required. For single persons only. Wireless internet for $5 for week.
UPTOWN HOSTEL (212) 666-0559 239 Lennox Avenue New York, NY 10027 Fax: (212) 663-5000 www.uptownhostel.com info@uptownhostel.com	**Rooms** Single $35 Double $55 **Dorms** 4 – 6 Beds $20 Shared bathroom for all rooms	Features a living room and residents have access to a stove and refrigeratior located on the second floor.

Short-Term Accommodations (W&M)

Name	Daily Rates	Notes
UNION SQUARE INN (212) 614-0500 209 East 14th Street New York, NY 10003 Fax: (212) 614-0512 www.unionsquareinn.com unionsquareinn@nyinns.com	**Rooms** **w / private bathrooms** Single $139 Double $159 – $179	24 hour bellman service. Weekend rates may be $10 or $20 higher than midweek rates.
VANDERBILT YMCA (212) 912-2500 224 East 47th Street New York, NY 10017 Fax: (212) 752-0210 www.ymcanyc.org ecolon@ymcanyc.org	Single $89 Double $100	TV, air conditioning, housekeeping services, use of safe-deposit boxes, 24-hour security, room service, and luggage storage. YMCA facilities also included. Maximum stay: 25 days.
WEST END STUDIOS (212) 662-6000 850 West End Avenue New York, NY 10025 Fax: (212) 865-0506 www.westendstudios.com westendstudios@aol.com	**Rooms** **w / shared bath** Single $89 – $99 Double $106 – $112 Triple $142 Quad $220 **w / private bath** Single $151	No credit cards. Maximum stay: 7 days.
WEST SIDE YMCA (212) 875-4100 5 West 63rd Street New York, NY 10023 Fax: (212) 875-4291 www.ymcanyc.org/westside wsguestrooms@ymcanyc.org	Single $64 Double $75 Triple $89 Shared bathroom for all rooms	TV in each room. Handicapped accessible. Maximum stay: 25 days.

Residences & Apartments (W&M)

Name	Daily Rates	Notes
CATHEDRAL GARDENS (800) 297-4694 (212) 977-9099 217 Manhattan Avenue New York, NY 10025 Fax: (212) 727-7284 www.studenthousing.org reservations@studenthousing.org	Rates from $3,300 – $7,600 per semester	*EHS Residence.* Residences are furnished with cooking and laundry facilities. Short term (less than four months) are available. Handicapped accessible; elevators provided in each residence.
CHELSMORE APARTMENTS (212) 924-7991 205 West 15th Street New York, NY 10011 Fax: (212) 727-7284 www.chelsmore.com reservations@chelsmore.com	$2,200+ / month	Long-term stays only (1 month or more). All apartments are furnished. Low vacancy rate. Call for availability. Total capacity: 100 apartments.
CLARK STREET RESIDENCE (800) 297-4694 (212) 977-9099 55 Clark Street Brooklyn, NY 11201 Fax: (212) 727-7284 www.studenthousing.org reservations@studenthousing.org	Rates from $3,300 – $7,600 per semester	*EHS Residence.* Residences are furnished with cooking and laundry facilities. Short term (less than four months) are available. Handicapped accesible; elevators provided in each residence.
DE HIRSCH RESIDENCE (212) 415-5650 (800) 858-4692 1395 Lexington Avenue New York, NY 10128 Fax: (212) 415-5578 http://www.dehirsch.com dehirsch@92ndsty.org	**30 days or longer** Current monthly rates: Large Single $1,550 Single $1,450 Double $1,250 Small Double $1,150 per person rate **For stays of 30 – 45 days (January to August)** Large Single $80 per day Single $75 per day Double $60 per person per day Small Double $50 per person per day	Fully furnished single and double rooms with shared bathrooms are available for periods of 30 days or longer. The residence has weekly maid service, kitchen and laundry room on each floor and 24-hour security. The residence also offers access to the Y's Buttenwieser Library (which has computers with internet access) and reduced or free admission to many of The Y's concerts and lectures. Fall semester bookings are for the entire fall semester only; September 1, 2009 – December 31, 2009. If you depart prior to December 31 you will be required to pay the rent through December 31. For stays of 30 – 45 days it is a nightly rate applies.

Residences & Apartments (W&M)

Name	Daily Rates	Notes
EAST SIDE RESIDENCE (800) 297-4694 224 East 47th Street New York, NY 10017 Fax: (212) 727-7284 www.studenthousing.org reservations@studenthousing.org	Rates from $3,300 – $7,600 per semester	*EHS Residence.* Residences are furnished with cooking and laundry facilities. Short term (less than four months) are available. Handicapped accesible; elevators provided in each residence.
EDUCATIONAL HOUSING SERVICES (EHS) STUDENT HOUSING CENTER (800) 297-4694 31 Lexington Avenue New York, NY 10010 www.studenthousing.org reservations@studenthousing.org	Rates from $3,300 – $7,600 per semester	Locations available in Brooklyn and Manhattan. Residences are furnished with cooking and laundry facilities. Short term (less than four moths) are available. Handicapped accesible; elevators provided in each residence. (Please refer to individual listings for contact information)
FSL SCHOLARSHIPS FOUNDATION NY STUDENT RESIDENCES AT MANHATTAN SCHOOL OF MUSIC (212) 629-7300 134 Claremont Avenue New York, NY 10027 Fax: (212) 736-7950 dhenning@studygroup.com	**Daily** Single $95 Shared Rooms $85 **Weekly** Single $378 Shared Rooms $295	Shared rooms contain a bed, desk, chair, wardrobe and chest of drawers. Facilities include shared shower and restrooms on each floor, wheel chair access, internet access and 24 hour security. Cafeteria on site. Student lounge with a large screen TV, DVD or video player. Minimum stay: 1 week.
INTERNATIONAL HOUSE (212) 316-8400 500 Riverside Drive New York, NY 10027 Fax: (212) 316-1827 www.ihouse-nyc.org admissions@ihouse-nyc.org	**Monthly** Single $748 – $1,245 Apartment $1,466 – $1,986	Open to full-time graduate students only during academic year; undergraduates welcome in summer. Application necessary for stays of 30 days or more. Handicapped accessible.
MARYMOUNT MANHATTAN COLLEGE RESIDENCE (800) 297-4694 231 East 55th Street New York, N 10022 Fax: (212) 727-7284 www.studenthousing.org reservations@studenthousing.org	Rates from $3,300 – $7,600 per semester	*EHS Residence.* Residences are furnished with cooking and laundry facilities. Short term (less than four months) are available. Handicapped accesible; elevators provided in each residence.

Residences & Apartments (W&M)

Name	Daily Rates	Notes
NEW YORKER (800) 297-4694 481 Eighth Avenue New York, NY 10001 Fax: (212) 727-7284 www.studenthousing.org reservations@studenthousing.org	Rates from $3,300 – $7,600 per semester	*EHS Residence.* Residences are furnished with cooking and laundry facilities. Short term (less than four months) are available. Handicapped accesible; elevators provided in each residence.
PENINGTON FRIENDS HOUSE (212) 673-1730 215 East 15th Street New York, NY 10003 www.penington.org peningtonfriends@yahoo.com	**Single** Monthly $883 – $1,479 Daily $85 Each additional person: $40 fee Shared bathroom for all rooms	Operated by Quakers, residents have housework. Breakfast and dinner are included (except Saturday). Rooms have phones with free unlimited calling, air conditioning. Laundry facility, cable facility with VRR/DVD player. Rear garden/patio.
PLIMPTON HALL RESIDENCE (800) 297-4694 1235 Amsterdam Avenue New York, NY 10027 Fax: (212) 727-7284 www.studenthousing.org reservations@studenthousing.org	Rates from $3,300 – $7,600 per semester	*EHS Residence.* Residences are furnished with cooking and laundry facilities. Short term (less than four months) are available. Handicapped accesible; elevators provided in each residence.
POLYTECHNIC UNIVERSITY (718) 260-4160 6 Metrotech Center Brooklyn, NY 11201 Fax: (718) 260-4195 www.poly.edu/residence/ summerhousing@poly.edu	**Suites** Double $40 Single $45 **Apartments** Double $55 Single $65	Accommodation available during the summer from June 1 to August 15. Amenities include: DirectTV cable access, internet access and laundry facilities, bed linens can be bought starting at $10. **Summer Residency only.**
SARA'S NY HOMESTAY (212) 564-5979 53 West 36th Street New York, NY 10018 Fax: (212) 564-0475 www.sarahomestay.com sara@sarahomestay.com	**Four weeks** $950 (discounts available for stays of 12 weeks or more) Cost for the second person 50% above price of single.	Private room with self served breakfast, sharing apartment or house with a family or a roommate. Shared bathrooms or private bathrooms available. Furnished apartments for individuals also available. $100 registration fee. Airport pick-up and drop-off available. Maximum stay: 7 nights minimum, up to four years.

Name	Daily Rates	Notes
ST. GEORGE RESIDENCE (212) 977-9099 (800) 297-4694 100 Henry Street Brooklyn, NY 11201 www.studenthousing.org reservations@studenthousing.org	**Per semester** Single $6,200 Double $4,650 Large Double $5,250 $150 membership fee; Summer rates available	*EHS Residence.* Residences are furnished with cooking and laundry facilities. Short term (less than four months) are available. Handicapped accesible; elevators provided in each residence.
TOWERS AT CCNY (800) 297-4694 401 West 130th Street New York, NY 10027 Fax: (212) 727-7284 www.studenthousing.org reservations@studenthousing.org	Rates from $3,300 – $7,600 per semester	*EHS Residence.* Residences are furnished with cooking and laundry facilities. Short term (less than four months) are available. Handicapped accesible; elevators provided in each residence.

Residences & Apartments (Women Only)

Name	Daily Rates	Notes
THE BRANDON (212) 496-6901 340 West 85th Street New York, NY 10024 Fax: (646) 505-0140 www.thebrandon.org Brandon@voa-gny.org	**Rooms w / shared bathroom** Daily $80 Monthly $1,023 – $1,218 **w / private baths** Monthly $1,218 $40 female guest fee	Furnished rooms include breakfast and dinner. Housekeeping service, linens, kitchen, refrigerator and laundry and ironing facilities. Lending library and TV room. 24-hour attendants at front desk. Building has elevator. Rehearsal space and piano. Application and interview. Minimum stay: 3 days.
CENTRO MARIA RESIDENCE (212) 581-5273 539 West 54th Street New York, NY 10019 Fax: (212) 307-5687 cenmariany@mindspring.com	**Weekly** Single $200 Double $175	Curfew: 11:30 p.m. Sunday – Thursday; 12 midnight Friday and Saturday. Breakfast and dinner included; Saturday breakfast only. Single women only, 18 – 29 years. Minimum stay: one month. 5 year maximum. $100 non-refundable registration fee.
EL CARMELO RESIDENCE (212) 242-8224 249 West 14th Street New York, NY 10010 Fax: (212) 242-7333 newyork.ctsj@carmelitastsj.org	Call for pricing 3 month stay in a double: $145 / week	Letter of recommendation required. Curfew: Sunday – Thursday 11 p.m.; Friday – Saturday 12 midnight. Breakfast and dinner included in rates. Meals are Monday – Friday only; ages 18 – 35. Minimum of 3 weeks and maximum of 13 weeks.

Residences & Apartments (Woman Only)

Name	Daily Rates	Notes
JEANNE D'ARC RESIDENCE (212) 989-5952 253 West 24th Street New York, NY 10011 www.cdpkentucky.org/5g.html jeannedarc_jeanne@yahoo.com	**Short term stay** Double $350 / month **Year long stay** Single $350/month Double $320/month	Applicants must provide employer, character references and a doctor's letter and be 18-40 years old. Call for application. Laundry, drink machine, kitchen and dining room available. Maximum stay: up to ten years. Other fees may apply for computer use, etc.
JUDSON POST HALL YWCA (718) 875-1190 ext. 223 30 Third Avenue Brooklyn, NY 11217 Fax: (718) 858-5731 www.ywcabklyn.org/ rordonez@ywcabklyn.org	**Daily** Small $55 Large w / private bath $90 **Monthly** $710	$20/month for phone. Large communal kitchen, community lounges, laundry facility, internet access and handicapped accessible. TV available on each floor. Roof top garden. 24 hour security. On site maintenance. Key deposite $20. Reference letter required.
MARKLE EVANGELINE RESIDENCE (212) 242-2400 123 West 13th Street New York, NY 10011 Fax: (212) 229-2801 www.themarkle.org/	**Monthly** Single $1,275 – $1,375 Double $1,070 – $1,620 Quad $920 – $940	Women ages 18 – 35. Rooms furnished with bed, dresser, desk and chair, lamp, linens and towels. Houskeeping and laundry facilities available. Roof-top garden. Application available online. Monday – Friday breakfast and dinner included. Weekends and holidays, breakfast and lunch included. Full time security. Minimum stay: 3 months.
SACRED HEART (212) 929-5790 432 West 20th Street New York, NY 10011 Fax: (212) 924-0891 www.sacredheartresidence. com/ info@sacredheartresidence.com	Daily $50 Weekly $240 If you stay a month or more, you must pay $960 in advance.	Women 18 to 30 years old. Non-refundable $50 deposit to guarantee reservation. Breakfast and dinner are served Monday through Friday. Curfew: Sunday to Thursday 11:00 p.m.; Friday and Saturday midnight.
ST. MARY'S RESIDENCE (212) 249-6850 225 East 72nd Street New York, NY 10021 Fax: (212) 249-4336 stmarysres72@aol.com	**Weekly (from 2 – 11 weeks)** $225 **(from 12+ weeks)** $190 Shared bathroom for all rooms	Smoke free building. Kitchen on each floor and lounge available. Laundry facility and maid service. Write to Lisa Rodriguez to get on waiting list.

Residences & Apartments (Men Only)

Name	Daily Rates	Notes
KOLPING HOUSE (212) 369-6647 165 East 88th Street New York, NY 10128 Fax: (212) 987-5652 www.kolpingny.org residence@kolpingny.org	Daily $65 Weekly $205 $65.00 non-refundable registration fee	Students need letter from parents guaranteeing payment. Men ages 18 – 35. Monday – Friday one meal a day included (lunch or dinner). Reservations should be made three months in advance. Passport and ID required.

Notes

Notes

Notes

Notes

Notes

Notes

Notes

Notes

New York University
Office for International Students and Scholars

www.nyu.edu/oiss